Naleli Morojele
Women Political Leaders in Rwanda and South Africa

Naleli Morojele

Women Political Leaders in Rwanda and South Africa
Narratives of Triumph and Loss

Barbara Budrich Publishers
Opladen • Berlin • Toronto 2016

A CIP catalogue record for this book is available from
Die Deutsche Bibliothek (The German Library)

© 2016 by Barbara Budrich Publishers, Opladen, Berlin & Toronto
www.barbara-budrich.net

ISBN   978-3-8474-0745-4
eISBN 978-3-8474-0905-2

Die Deutsche Bibliothek – CIP-Einheitsaufnahme
Ein Titeldatensatz für die Publikation ist bei der Deutschen Bibliothek erhältlich.

Verlag Barbara Budrich Ⓑⁱ Barbara Budrich Publishers
Stauffenbergstr. 7. D-51379 Leverkusen Opladen, Germany

86 Delma Drive. Toronto, ON M8W 4P6 Canada
www.barbara-budrich.net

Jacket illustration by Bettina Lehfeldt, Germany – www.lehfeldtgraphic.de
Editing: Alison Romer, Lancaster, England
Typographical editing: Anja Borkam, Jena, Germany
Printed in Europe on acid-free paper by
paper&tinta, Warsaw

Acknowledgements

Women Political Leaders in Rwanda and South Africa: Narratives of Triumph and Loss came about from earlier research that I had conducted for my Master of Arts dissertation at the Centre for Africa Studies at the University of the Free State. I would like to express my gratitude to all of the participants that I interviewed. Their willingness to share their stories has been invaluable. This book would not have been possible without their openness to share their experiences, some of which are personal and intimate. I believe that it is extremely important to record the stories of women, such as these, as a way of creating an inclusive history of society that considers women's experiences. We need their stories to be able to reflect on how far women have come in terms of our status in society, but also to remind us to steadfastly continue walking the road that they have paved for us, remembering that we still have a long way to go to create equal societies.

Not only the participants, this book is the result of the assistance and efforts of numerous individuals and organisations, that I would like to recognise here.

The writing of this book was made possible through the funding provided by the University of the Free State to Trauma, Forgiveness and Reconciliation Studies. They funded the costs of the research itself, but also enabled me to dedicate the time needed to write this book.

I'd especially like to recognise and express my gratitude to Prof. Pumla Gobodo-Madikizela, without whom the research, funding and writing of this book would not have been possible. Her support has greatly contributed not only to the logistical aspects of this book, but also to the development of the content itself. Having her as my MA supervisor has been an inspiring experience, and I attribute my continuing development as a scholar and researcher to her guidance.

For her assessment, feedback and guidance on the earlier stage of my research, I'd like to thank Prof. Hannah Britton, who has also written the foreword in this book. Her own work has been instrumental in my understanding and the development of my ideas regarding women and politics. Her feedback on my work has been immensely useful and encouraging.

I'd also like to thank The Centre for Gender Studies, College of Arts and Social Sciences, University of Rwanda, and Dr. Jolly Rubagiza, who provided me with affiliation to be able to conduct my research in Rwanda, and also assisted me in securing participants in Rwanda. The Institute for Inclusive Security, Washington D.C., including Pari Farmani, also introduced me to some of the Rwandan participants.

I'd also like to thank the staff at Trauma, Forgiveness and Reconciliation Studies, particularly Mrs. Jo-Anne Naidoo, who assisted with the various paperwork, logistics and moral support to conduct the research for this book.

It's important for me to also make mention of my previous professors at Wheaton College, Massachusetts, though they have not been involved in this book. My academic interest in and passion for women's issues and gender equality developed during my undergraduate studies at Wheaton College. I would like to thank them for teaching me the language and critical thinking that is so needed to understand women's status (and other social issues) in society today. I'd especially like to thank Prof. Brenda Wyss, Prof. Kim Miller, Prof. Kathryn Tomasek, and Prof. Russell Williams.

Finally, a deep appreciation to my family, Cecily and Redvers Anderson, for their love, sacrifices and immeasurable support. Their assistance, in various ways, has enabled me to dedicate myself to my work. My grandparents, Andy and Ellen Anderson, who have been examples of what a vision and strong work ethic can achieve.

Contents

Foreword

The field of women and politics has advanced significantly in the last twenty years, both in terms of scope and methods. We now have remarkable insights into electoral strategies that benefit women's representation, new understandings about the impact and role of women in government, and a growing awareness of the cascade effect of gender-friendly policies from country to country. In the midst of all of this new information, we often forget that some of the strongest contributions in this field have come from understanding the women leaders themselves as political actors, what brought them to office, and their vision and challenges. Naleli Morojele's work is precisely this type of contribution. *Women Political Leaders in Rwanda and South Africa: Narratives of Triumph and Loss* is one of the most original and vital contributions to these very core topics in several years. Her work reminds us of the value and importance of reflective, engaging partnerships with women leaders and what those types of partnerships can bring to our understanding of leadership, conflict, and peacemaking.

Morojele's work is a thoroughly original effort to further our field through comparative field research partnering with women leaders in *both* Rwanda and South Africa. Comparative field-based projects like this are rare, and Ms. Morojele has captured some of the most engaging and provocative findings for us to consider. After a thorough discussion of the existing literature on both South Africa and Rwanda, Ms. Morojele then presents original interview research with leading women in politics in both countries. It is a pleasure to see two such interesting cases – Rwanda and South Africa –compared so directly in terms of women and leadership. These two cases individually have been two of the most studied and discussed post-conflict cases in Africa, but rarely are they compared. As Ms. Morojele discusses, the cases have some important similarities, including conflicts ending in the same year, a national commitment to include women in post-conflict political leadership, and efforts toward national reconciliation and building a lasting peace. They also have many key differences – different languages, different types of conflict (genocide versus struggle for national liberation), different legacies of colonization, different foreign interests, and different economies and levels of development. It is rare to see these two cases brought into direct comparison, and her findings are provocative.

Rather than focusing exclusively on women from one branch of government, Ms. Morojele speaks with women legislators and members of the cabinet and bureaucracy – a rare scope of leadership capturing both policy-making and policy implementation. She also shares extensive information from her interviews – allowing the women to speak for themselves. This is increasingly scarce in our field, which is becoming dominated by more quantitative studies covering dozens of countries. Given the extensive interview material presented in this manuscript, scholars will be able to use her work to find new patterns and ideas in their own work. It is clear from the insight and intimacy of the interviews that these women leaders had great confidence in Ms. Morojele and what her work would mean. It is one of the greatest tributes to her work and her process.

Women Political Leaders in Rwanda and South Africa: Narratives of Triumph and Loss also demonstrates Ms. Morojele's substantial interdisciplinary strengths – as she addresses some key concepts from political science, women's studies, and African studies. She has important and original ideas about electoral systems, electoral strategies, and institutional systems - that are the core of political science. Indeed, she comprehensively covers the literature and scholarship in this field, and this work will be invaluable for new and emerging scholars because of this solid overview. She engages some of the eternal questions of our field: Does having more women in office matter? What are the limitations and strengths of quotas and symbolic representation? How are women elected through quotas able to counteract the stereotypes of 'window-dressing'? How do women challenge patronage, authoritarianism, and party politics while advancing their political agenda and women's issues?

Ms. Morojele also brings focus to some substantial issues in gender studies including gender and education, gender and literacy, feminization of poverty, and reproductive health. She pays particular attention to why education is so important for women personally, professionally, and politically. She also does not shy away from examining the continued gender-biases in education globally and how this has compounded women's vulnerability through their lifetime.

Feminist scholars and political leaders will find great value in this book's rich discussion of the "three shifts" that women politicians have to face – marriage, motherhood, and work. She provocatively challenges us to rethink the feminist critique of the third shift. The voices of the women leaders she interviews squarely challenge the ideas of a work/life balance – specifically recognizing that the choice between politics and family is a false choice. Ms. Morojele asks us to expect more of society, and she makes a strong case that women can and should have meaningful roles in politics and still be deeply engaged in family and relationships. To do any less underestimates women and the struggle themselves.

Women Political Leaders in Rwanda and South Africa: Narratives of Triumph and Loss covers some of the most original and important material I have seen on how women leaders view their national conflicts and the processes peace making

– truly bringing force to the idea of triumph and loss. Their narratives are moving and are rich in detail and insight. We learn about the sacrifices they made, the impact of the conflict on their lives, and how they approached the struggle and rebuilding their countries. Ms. Morojele has given us provocative material that can shift our understanding of both of women's leadership and the impact of politics on women's lives. She has a strength of analysis that give us a clear grasp of the significance of her findings, while at the same time allowing us to make our own conclusions and draw our own insights from these thoughtful and reflective narratives. You cannot leave the pages of this book unmoved or unchanged. I commend this work and what it will offer us for years to come.

Prof. H.E. Britton
Director of the Center for the Study of Injustice at the Institute of Policy & Social Research at the University of Kansas

Introduction

In early 2015 Rwanda had the world's highest representation of women in a national legislature, with women holding 63.8% of the seats in the lower house. South Africa had the tenth highest representation level with 41.5% of seats in the lower house (Inter-Parliamentary Union 2015). These figures sharply contrast with those of just over two decades earlier. Before 1994, formal positions in politics and government in Rwanda and South Africa were largely closed to women. During Apartheid in South Africa women represented just 2.8% of the national parliament (Gobodo-Madikizela 2005). Before 1994 women were also extremely under-represented in Rwanda. In 1992 there were only three women ministers and twelve women Ministers of Parliament (MPs) out of a total of 70 (Sharlach 1999). Rwanda and South Africa's 2015 representation figures also sharply contrast with the current global average of 22.2% women's representation (Inter-Parliamentary Union 2015). For these reasons, Rwanda and South Africa are excellent case studies of women and politics. They enable us to understand how to quickly increase women's political representation levels, as well as to understand what this means for politics, and women's status in society.

A great portion of the literature on women and politics in these countries has asked the question of how it came to be that women's representation levels could rise so significantly over a short period of time e.g. (Tripp n.d.; Geisler 2000; Yoon 2001; Hassim 2004; Ballington 1998; Britton 2002b). A second portion of the literature has interrogated what these women bring to politics in terms of substantive representation; what they have (or have not) achieved in institutional and legislative outcomes for women (e.g. Britton 2002a; Coffé 2012; Goetz 1998; Gouws 1996).

This book aims to contribute to this discourse, as well as expand on it. Through interviews with eleven women who have held formal political leadership positions since 1994 in Rwanda and South Africa, I explore the journeys and experiences that have led them to formal politics. I explore their social and political impact, as well as their challenges. Finally, I explore their early experiences as children and young adults, and their experiences of marriage and motherhood as political figures. All of this is to suggest three things. Firstly, while the women that I interviewed occupy important positions and are advantaged in certain ways, many of their experiences are no different from the ordinary women that they represent. I also suggest that there were specific moments and experiences in their lives that have continued to influence their political priorities today. Lastly, I will show that they have clear beliefs regarding women's interests, based off their experiences, and that these have influenced their politics, but more than that, they are interested in representing all people, not only women.

Women in Politics

Since the 1990's there have been countries in which women's representation levels have increased drastically over a short period of time. These countries are known as fast-track countries (Tripp & Kang 2008: 338; Dahlerup & Freidenvall 2006: 27). Sharp increases in women's representation often occur in post-conflict periods where normal gender roles have been disrupted and women have taken on traditionally male roles. Families are divided and women take up leadership within the home and provide for the family. This has happened in countries such as Mozambique, Uganda, South Africa and Rwanda, amongst others (Uwineza & Pearson 2009). Not only are the gender roles disrupted, but so are the social and political institutions. It is for this reason that the post-conflict transition can present unique opportunities for women to access formal political positions, as this is a period that is more flexible and receptive to drastic changes (Debusscher & Ansoms 2013; Goetz et al. 2009; Kantengwa 2010).

Why is important to examine women in politics? Questions regarding women's roles during this precious transition period from conflict to peace include; do women act differently and bring different skills than men do? If so, what are their contributions, and how do these enhance transformation? (Gobodo-Madikizela 2005). 80% of women MPs who participated in a survey conducted by the Inter-Parliamentary Union in 1999 felt that, in general, women do change politics and improve public perceptions of politics. They also felt that women and men perceive politics and society differently, and a true democracy requires the participation of men and women. Many modern African states, in particular, have fought liberation wars and an African strand of feminism has arisen within this context. This feminism holds that women's interests should be advanced within politics and the state, not only in the churches, academia, etc. (Gaidzanwa 2013). While the conflicts in some states are over, such as in Rwanda and South Africa, women have not been fully emancipated from various forms of inequalities and oppressions. For this reason, it is important to continually examine the status of women. In the area of women and politics we should explore the relationship between women and politics and what this means for society in general. In this book I explore not only women politicians, but I do so in relation to their

12

contexts, as well as try to draw a link between their experiences and ordinary women.

The State of Women

There are regional disparities in terms of women's social rights. These include rights to travel, obtain passports, initiate divorce, equal inheritance, etc. It is found that women's social discrimination is highest in the Middle East, followed by Sub-Saharan Africa. In accessing economic rights, such as equal pay for equal work, job security etc. Sub-Saharan Africa has the highest proportion of discrimination against women (A.M. Goetz et al. 2009).

In Sub-Saharan Africa in the period between 1999 and 2005, just 29% of married women had a final say in their own health care, 13% on large purchases, and only 35% had a say in daily purchases. Of unmarried women; 51% had no say over their own health care, 59% had no say over large purchases, and 43% had no say in daily purchases (A.M. Goetz et al. 2009). These figures are alarming. They indicate the dire status of women as second class citizens, and the patriarchal, gendered oppression that they experience on a daily basis.

However, research shows that when women are in positions to make decisions, they make those that benefit families and children. For example, in development it has been shown that if we invest in women, children are more likely to benefit than if we invest in men. Similarly, there are long term benefits to the health and education of children if women's health and education is improved (Elizabeth Powley 2006). Fester (2007) makes an important point on this argument in the development field though. That is; why are we framing improving the lives of women as development issues? Shouldn't we rather take the position that women have the right to have better lives; not just as a means to an end, but as an end in and of itself?

The importance of examining women and politics is evidenced by the fact that women's activism has shown that men and women experience governance failures differently(A.M. Goetz et al. 2009). In other words, women are in the best position to know what other women require from politics and the state; men and women's experiences in this area are different and so men are not able to know (never mind represent) the needs of women. In terms of the argument for increasing women's representation in politics; many women politicians around the world feel that women have special skills and have more humanity in their politics

13

(Waring et al 2000).

Political and Conflict History

Before Rwanda was colonised, there were social differences in which the politically dominant clans were those who owned cattle and competed for domination over the settled agricultural populations. However, during colonisation the Germans, Belgians and Catholic Church subscribed to the theory of Hamitic racial superiority of the Tutsi, and cemented and made rigid the fluid divisions that existed. In 1930 the Belgian colonialists created identity cards that cemented their constructed ethnic divisions into Hutu, Tutsi and Twa. Before these relationships were not always adversarial. People lived together, sharing the same culture and language, and relationships were more individualised than based on ethnicity. The process of Rwanda's independence from colonial rule began in the 1950s, but it was through a coup d'état, which was supported by the Belgians, that Rwanda became a Republic under majority Hutu rule. Hutu prefects were appointed to take over from former Tutsi chiefs and sub-chiefs. During this process the Tutsi were victimised and approximately 100 000 refugees, mostly those who supported the monarchy, went to Burundi, Congo, Uganda and Tanzania. This first group of exiles would stage border raids into Rwanda, which were ineffective, but ultimately helped the Hutu leadership to propagate Anti-Tutsi prejudices. With these raids there were reprisal massacres against those Tutsis who had remained in the country, which created subsequent waves of non-political refugees out of Rwanda. The massacres against Tutsis in 1963 were called genocide by some in the international community (Long 2012; van der Meeren 1996). The Rwandan Patriotic Front (RPF), Rwanda's liberation movement and current ruling party, was founded in exile by some Rwandan refugees in the 1980's (Reed 1996).

Before the 1994 genocide Rwanda was governed by a single party and the dictatorship of President Habyarimana. In 1989 opposition parties began to demand liberalisation, and this occurred in the context of a civil society and international community that called for democratisation. In 1991 a civil war began when the RPF attacked Rwanda from outside the country. During the war Habyarimana faced military loses to the RPF as well as internal and international pressure, and was forced to the negotiating table. The subsequent 1993 Arusha Peace Accords outlined a plan for the country to transition to democratic elections and multi-party politics. This transition abruptly ended in April 1994 when Habyarimana was killed when his plane was shot down. Hutu extremists took over government and initiated the genocide against Tutsi and moderate Hutu. During this time the RPF reinitiated its military actions against the government army. The genocide and war ended when the RPF drove the Hutu government and extremist militias into exile, with about 2 million refugees (J. E. Burnet 2008).

Since then Rwanda has been praised for the rapid pace at which it has been able to rebuild itself, and there has been praise for the government for the delivery of services such as education and health. Amongst its achievements include low corruption levels, economic growth and a strong modernisation program to move Rwanda from a low-income to medium-income country. The RPF-led government has appointed women to important positions in government and the judiciary, women have been mainstreamed in the party itself, and there are reserved seats for women in the national parliament (Debusscher & Ansoms 2013). The RPF's inclusion of women in decision-making positions arises out of their having been influenced by Uganda's policies of women's inclusion while they were refugees, as well the constitutional and representational success in South Africa (Elizabeth Powley 2006).

During the 1994 genocide Women in Rwanda experienced rape as a weapon of war, sexual slavery, having their children killed, fighting as soldiers, hiding from perpetrators, as well as fleeing pogroms before 1994, etc. They not only had these experiences as a result of their Tutsi ethnicity or Tutsi association, but also because of their gender. Beyond these violent experiences, their resilience in rebuilding Rwanda speaks to their strength and power, and has strongly influenced Rwandan society's current ideas about women (Herndon & Randell 2013). A Rwandan leader, Chair of Parliament's Human Rights Committee, said, 'More than men, women are the victims of the war. They have different priorities to those of men...Women have faced discrimination so they want to put a stop to discrimination. All of this will contribute to preventing another genocide,' (Quoted in Herndon & Randell 2013: 79).

Unfortunately, the genocide aggravated poverty levels, and more than 68% of women live below the poverty line (Kantengwa 2010). There is still extreme poverty in Rwanda, especially in the rural areas. Despite the rights that women have gained since 1994, those who work in the markets report still being exploited by their husbands (Herndon & Randell 2013). Indeed, Rwanda remains a mostly patriarchal society (Kantengwa 2010). The good news is that in 2003 Rwanda elected 48.8% women to its lower house in the national parliament, thereby having the highest representation of women in the world. In 2008 women won 56% of seats in the lower house, maintaining its global lead. This is evidence of a sustained commitment to women's representation (Uwineza & Pearson 2009). What this means for all Rwandan women I interrogate in the following chapters.

As mentioned earlier, South African women's legislative success was an influence on Rwanda. Just a few days before the genocide in Rwanda began, South African women won 26% of the seats in the national parliament (Uwineza & Pearson 2009). South African women were very active in the struggle against apartheid and they made important contributions both inside the country and outside in exile. Women were the first to take mass action against the Pass Laws in 1913 and did so again in the 1950's. In exile many women received military training which led to them having some power within the movement (Ginwala 1990; b. Britton 2002a; Hassim 2004). Women formed their own organisations, such as the Federation of South African Women (FSAW), which was established in 1953 and drafted the Women's Charter in 1954 (Anne Marie Goetz 1998). They also played important roles during the transition, not only through politics, but through the reconciliation process, such as commissioners, staff , and through witness testimony (especially testifying on behalf of other victims such as sons and husbands) at the Truth and Reconciliation Commission (Gobodo-Madikizela 2005).

Apartheid, and the systemised inequalities between the races, only became the law of the land in 1948, but before then Black people were already excluded from formal politics and were treated as second class citizens during British colonialism and the Union of South Africa. 'Apartheid' itself means separateness. In addition, Apartheid politics was a patriarchal system dominated by men (Gobodo-Madikizela 2005). Non-violent protest against the Apartheid regime ended in the 1960's after the Sharpeville Massacre where peaceful protesters against the Pass where shot by the police, killing 69 people. The government then banned the ANC (African National Congress) and other anti-Apartheid organisations. This led to the ANC adopting an armed struggle through Umkhonto we Sizwe (MK) (Graybill 2001). Some ANC women also received military training in MK, especially after 1976 (Geisler 2000; Hassim 2004).

The Apartheid state was a brutal regime that used violence against civilians (such as in the Sharpeville Massacre) and Anti-Apartheid activists. It used many types of interrogation including torture and solitary confinement without trial. Torture methods included physical assaults, sleep deprivation, and being forced to stand for long periods of time. Methods of torturing women were more gendered, such as the use of rape, forced intercourse, rape with objects, vaginal examinations and body searches. Women's motherhood was also exploited; children were removed from them or their children's lives were threatened as a torture method (Graybill 2001).

Despite women's important contributions to the Anti-Apartheid struggle, they were considered the 'silent backbone' of the movement (Britton 2002a: 44). However, during the 1980's women's emancipation began to be addressed more within the ANC in exile and other movements within the country (Geisler 2000; Hassim 2004). For example, in the 1980's the United Democratic Front (UDF) was formed, and comprised of about 400 anti-Apartheid organisations. Albertina Sisulu, who was one of the founders of the FSAW, was a co-president. There were many women's organisations that were affiliated to the UDF, and they were able to persuade the leadership of the UDF to have non-sexism as one of its principles (Geisler 2000)[1]. The earlier limited acknowledgement of South African women's status was not unusual. Around the world women's liberation has taken a back seat to national liberation. However, in 1990 the National Executive Committee (NEC) of the ANC issued a statement acknowledging that women's liberation would not be a secondary effect of national liberation or of socialism. It stated that women's emancipation needed to be directly addressed within the ANC, the democratic movement and within society (Geisler 2000; Hassim 2004).

In 1991 South African women's organisations formed the Women's National Coalition (WNC), which united around the common interest of ensuring that women were included in the transitional process and the shaping of a new South Africa (Britton 2002b). South African women had learned from the independence of neighbouring countries such as Namibia and Zimbabwe that gender equality and women's representation would not happen unless they formed a united front and pushed for representation. One of their demands was that women had to be included in positions of decision-making power (Geisler 2000; Britton 2002b). Many of the women who arrived in parliament in 1994 arrived through the ANC candidate list and had been involved in the Anti-Apartheid movement and this women's movement. During the first democratic elections the ANC was the only party to use women's rights as a campaign topic (Geisler 2000).

Despite the phenomenal achievements of South Africa, particularly the WNC and ANC, in ensuring that women were included in the transition and in democratic governance, gender inequality is still a pervasive problem in South African society. Change will not be drastic or swift because it is approached from a reform basis, rather than a revolutionary basis. South Africa's women continue to face patriarchy, gender-based violence, and poverty. They are still not treated as full citizens (Britton 2002a). Unfortunately, Black women are still the poorest

---

[1] For more about women's structures and roles in the ANC in exile Hassim (2004) provides a historical analysis, including how women lobbied to have the ANC include non-sexism as one of its core principles.

17

demographic in South Africa and those who are employed are mostly in low-paying jobs, such as domestic service; one of the far-reaching consequences of the Apartheid system (Graybill 2001).

International Women's Movement

Women's increased representation in Rwanda and South Africa have not occurred in isolation. A strong international women's movement has been campaigning to have women represented in positions of decision-making power. There have been many pivotal moments and instruments in this international women's movement. There was the United Nations Decade for Women which began in 1975, and included the call to have women equally included in governance. Many countries around the world have signed and ratified the Convention on the Elimination of All Forms of Discrimination Against Women (CEDAW) which is a United Nations (UN) treaty that was adopted in 1979. CEDAW is the achievement of the advocacy and mobilisation of women around the world and in the UN. CEDAW sets standards for national policy aimed at the eradication of discrimination against women. It calls for the reform of institutions and laws for women's rights, to have women and men equally represented in positions of political decision-making power, and to ensure that resources are made available to achieve those objectives. While many countries have ratified it, implementation results are mixed. Rwanda and South Africa have both ratified CEDAW (A.M. Goetz et al. 2009; Seager 2003). There is also the Beijing Declaration and Platform for Action (BPfA) which has been signed by all 189 of the states that participated at the United Nations Fourth World Conference on Women in Beijing in 1995. It called on governments to implement measures for women's equal participation in government (Dahlerup & Freidenvall 2006; Fallon et al. 2012). Many of the countries that adopted quotas after 1995, the year of the UN Conference on Women was held in Beijing, cite CEDAW and the (BPfA) as contributing factors (Tripp 2003). Women's representation is also one of the indicators of the Millennium Development Goals (Goetz et al. 2009).

Despite these various instruments, women's experiences of representation are not universal; rather, they are context specific and determined by a wide range of economic, political, and state factors (Burnet 2011). As indicated previously, Rwanda and South Africa have amongst the highest levels of women's representation in the world.

However, even within the Sub-Saharan region there is diversity in women's representation. More recently, Sub-Saharan Africa has provided interesting and sometimes paradoxical instances of gains in women's legislative impact. In 1997 the top ten countries in terms of women's representation did not include any African countries except for the Seychelles, which was seventh. By 2014 there were three African countries on the list, including Rwanda, Seychelles and Senegal. South Africa ranked eleventh. These countries represent exceptions (including Tanzania, Uganda and Zimbabwe in the top thirty countries represented) They are exceptions because the average Sub-Saharan African level of women's representation was just 22.1% in 2014 (Inter-Parliamentary Union 2005).

But are they exceptions in average women's rights + quality of life as a result?

Previous Literature

good phrase to use

The body of literature on women and politics is too extensive to summarise here.[2] However, within that genre there is a large body of work on women's legislative representation. This research investigates how women enter legislatures and what impact they have. The research mostly consists of western case studies, which offers little insights into other contexts (Devlin & Elgie 2008). The general research on women and political leadership has looked at the use of gender quotas in terms of what forms they take, their effects, and what kinds of countries are most likely to adopt them (Dahlerup 2007; Tripp 2003).

Other literature on the topic of women and politics is concerned with examining whether women's increased representation has an impact on legislation, and results have been mixed e.g. (Barnes & Burchard 2012; Bratton 2005). Yet newer work in the area is starting to make the argument that numbers are not the most important indicator of the impact of women's representation, rather it is better to consider how individuals act to make a change e.g (Celis et al. 2008; Childs & Krook 2009). Previous research on Rwanda and South Africa focuses on women's legislative impact, but also on how these countries have been able to attain the representation levels that they have.

---

[2] Kunovich et al (2007) provides one of the most comprehensive review articles on women and politics, but focusing on women's formal political participation. They find that the areas of research that should be expanded include understanding other ways that women can have political agency, to address intersectionality (the meeting of different identities), and also the need for more data collection.

Firstly, there is a large body of research that focuses on women's experiences of genocide in Rwanda e.g. (Hogg 2010; Maier 2013; Sharlach 1999). A separate body of work on women in Rwanda has asked whether their high level of representation has had an impact on legislation and women's lives. The findings are mixed, with some making the argument that Rwandan women cannot have a real impact as they are constrained by what some are calling an authoritarian regime (Tripp n.d.; Burnet 2008; Debusscher & Ansoms 2013). Other literature has made the argument that women political leaders are making a significant impact on Rwandan society, though with some challenges e.g. (Coffé 2012; Kantengwa, 2010; Powley 2005; Powley 2006; Uwineza & Pearson 2009). Others argue that there have been mixed results in terms of legislative and social impact (Devlin & Elgie 2008; Herndon & Randell 2013).

Similarly, research on women and politics in South Africa have explored the ways in which South Africa has been able to achieve the high representation levels that it has, including women's political and activist experiences during Apartheid (Ballington 1998; Britton 2002b; Hassim 2004). Some studies look at the successes and challenges that South Africa's women parliamentarians have experienced e.g. (Geisler 2000; Britton 2002a) as well as interrogating South Africa's commitment to women's rights e.g. (Fester 2007). While Mtintso (2003) conducted a study that questioned whether South African women's interests can ever be the same given the various identities they have which have been partly created by the divisions sown by the Apartheid system, complicating the discourse on who women politicians are meant to represent.

Beyond legislative impact, scholars have also been asking whether having women in visible positions of leadership has had an effect on the social perceptions of women. For example, a study conducted of Global North countries found that as women's representation increases, so too does the political participation of adolescent and adult women (Wolbrecht & Campbell 2007). In Rwanda, (Burnet 2011) conducted a study of both ordinary women and women in leadership and found that Rwandan women feel that have gained the respect of their communities, country, and some men as well.

The Inter- Parliamentary Union conducted a survey of almost 200 women politicians around the world, which it published in 1999. This survey has tried to achieve something similar to what I attempt to do here, but in different ways. The survey explores diverse women political leaders (including junior ministers and cabinet members) and on a range of topics, such as their family life, educational and professional backgrounds, their entries into politics, political instruments such as quotas, etc. However, the way in which the IPU survey differs from this book is that it was much broader, comprising 187 respondents from 65 countries, whereas

I interviewed 11 women in two countries. The size of the IPU's sample and research topics makes an in-depth analysis almost impossible, but it provides an excellent preliminary exploration and understanding of the topics pertaining to women political leaders.

In addition, the methodology used is different; mine consisted of original interviews and secondary sources, whereas the IPU was a survey completed independently by the respondents. Finally, our results are analysed differently. The IPU survey aggregates many responses into percentage numbers, it quotes some responses and at times compares different regions, and provides anecdotes from some countries. On the other hand, I try to paint a more detailed portrait of women political leaders by contextualising their responses, rather than trying to aggregate them. I also attempt to make linkages and comparisons between my two case studies, Rwanda and South Africa.

Conclusion

This book is not an exhaustive examination of all the issues pertaining women and politics, nor does it aim to make any conclusive findings. Rather, it is an attempt to contribute to the discussion about women in political leadership in Rwanda and South Africa, and it makes some suggestions on new ways of investigating and understanding women and political leadership.

Firstly, women politicians to some extent do represent the interests of women in Rwanda and South Africa. However, their impact is complicated, and influenced by many factors, many of which are at times out of their control, despite their influential positions. Secondly, while women politicians do occupy privileged positions, in many respects their life experiences are still affected by their gender in countries that still experience deep patriarchy. In other words, becoming a powerful woman does not make you a man. This is most evident by the challenges that they face in their personal lives, as I explore later. In addition, women politicians are not solely defined by their gender, and if we are to understand them, their impact, and what this means for ordinary women, we cannot try to force women politicians into the box of 'woman'. They are moulded by numerous experiences, such as their experiences of conflict, geographical and political dislocation, of racial/ethnic inequality, and class inequalities. This is not a new idea; rather I try here to show how these various identities play out once women receive the additional identity of 'politician'.

I attempt to contextualise the experiences and circumstances of the women that I interviewed. I explore who they are in relation to the average woman in their countries. By contextualising the experiences of the women that I interviewed, it also becomes clear that the women's experiences were intricately tied to the happenings in their countries, that through their stories we are able to construct a woman's history, as well as a gendered history of these countries, a shift from explaining history from only the eyes and experiences of men.

Chapter 1: Explaining Women's Representation: Quotas, Proportional Representation and Political Will

'I think that if you are treated in a society as a minority that has no power, that has no influence, that is marginalised as women are, we will not wait for a world that will not have patriarchy.'

In 1975 the United Nations Decade for Women began, and partly addressed issues of women's equality in governance. The issue of women's representation in decision-making bodies, such as national legislatures, was first advocated for by a global women's movement. One of the achievements of this women's movement was not only the United Nations Decade for Women, but also the Beijing Declaration and Platform for Action. This declaration requested that governments implement measures to enable women to have equal access to power and participation in decision-making structures (Dahlerup & Freidenvall 2006; Fallon et al. 2012). Since 1995 many nation states and regional and international structures have taken resolutions to increase women's legislative representation. These include the African Union (AU), the Economic Community of West African States (ECOWAS) and the Southern African Development Community (SADC) (Tripp 2003). These and others in the international community view gender quotas as one of the most critical instruments for increasing women's legislative representation in particular. The popularity of quotas is evidenced by the amount of countries that adopted them over a comparatively short period of time. From 1975 to 1985 only 4 countries introduced gender quotas. From 1995 (after the Beijing Declaration and Platform for Action) to 2005 more than 55 countries introduced quotas (Fallon et al. 2012). These countries are from diverse social, economic and political systems, and different levels of development (Dahlerup & Freidenvall 2006).

One element that appears to be most common amongst countries that have successfully implemented gender quotas and increased women's representation is the electoral system. To date various quantitative and qualitative studies indicate that quotas and proportional representation electoral systems are the most effective means for increasing women's representation. As a result of the increased global attention to women's political participation, and the importance of quotas and electoral systems for increasing women's legislative representation, there is a great wealth of scholarship and debate regarding the most effective types of quotas, the drawbacks of using quotas and the effectiveness of the proportional representation system (Ballington 1998; Dahlerup & Freidenvall

2006; Dahlerup 2007; Fallon et al. 2012; Krook, 2008; Kunovich et al. 2007; Tripp & Kang 2008; Tripp 2003).

Quotas

There are several reasons to explain the increased adoption of gender quotas around the world.[3] Firstly, women (both local and international) mobilised and advocated for the adoption of quotas. Secondly, political elites may adopt quotas to gain benefits associated with quotas, such as attracting women voters. Thirdly, quotas are advocated for by international norms and standards, as discussed above (Krook 2008). Rwanda and South Africa make use of gender quotas (Ballington 1998; Tripp 2003). Similarly, in Rwanda and South Africa there are several reasons put forth for the adoption of quotas.

Rwanda has constitutional reserved seats accounting for 30% of the national legislature. These were introduced in 2003 (Tripp 2003). With reserved seats 30% of the national parliamentary seats go to elected women and only women are allowed to contest and vote for these seats (Dahlerup 2007; Krook 2008). *The fact that the number of women in decision making positions has increased at this extent is based on the constitution, because the constitution institutionalised the quota, at least 30%, determine the composition of the parliament with at least 30% of women (Interview with the author, Kigali, 2013).*

One of the dangers of quotas is that they can be used by regimes as a means of legitimising themselves in accordance with international norms and standards and to win the loyalty of women constituents and candidates. This is one of the major criticisms of Rwanda's quotas, and its women politicians themselves. However, immediately after the genocide, before the constitutional quota was adopted, women took on leadership roles in reconciling and rebuilding the country (Tripp n.d.). What is interesting in the Rwandan case is that women's representation was comparatively high prior to the adoption of a gender quota. While quotas were adopted in 2003, women had joined the now ruling RPF before 1994, when it was a liberation movement. During the transitional government 46% of the parliamentary seats held by the RPF were held by women. From 1999, as part of Rwanda's 'Vision 2020' was the requirement to accelerate women's access to

[3] For a comprehensive study on the gender quotas and other variables (such as the influence of religion and democracy) see Tripp & Kang, 2008.

decision-making power (Kantengwa 2010). Therefore, the argument that Rwanda's women politicians are the tool of an authoritarian regime is overly-simplistic and, some would argue, incorrect.

In South Africa there are no special seats set-aside for women. It is the prerogative of the political parties to adopt and implement gender quotas and increase women candidates (Krook 2008). The implementation of quotas is largely due to the advocacy of a strong woman's movement in the early 1990's. During the transition from Apartheid to a democratic system, and during the Convention for a Democratic South Africa (CODESA) negotiations, the Women's League of the ANC initiated the Women's National Coalition (WNC) which encompassed numerous women's organisations from around the country. Amongst other things, the WNC demanded and received women's participation in the CODESA negotiations. Again, ANC women spearheaded this initiative (Geisler 2000; Goetz & Hassim 2003). *We raised it sharply within the ANC that there's just no way that men are going to be negotiating on our behalf; we have to be there. So we were included (Interview with author, Pretoria, 2013).* The WNC also decided that they did not want women to be excluded from government in the new regime, as had been the case in many other post-liberation African states. It therefore lobbied political parties to adopt gender quotas (Geisler 2000; Goetz & Hassim 2003). *And fortunately at that time there was a strong women's movement in South Africa, what we call the Women's National Coalition...and the women in the different parties negotiated, or made it a point that the question of gender equality be included in our Constitution and in everything we did. And I think that is why we have one of the best Constitutions in terms of gender, it was because of the ANC women who were the majority and the ANC as a whole...but also the other women in the other political parties who also pushed, even if minimally, but they did push (Interview with author, Pretoria, 2014).* As a result, South Africa has party quotas - though not all parties have adopted quotas. The ruling ANC currently has a 50% quota, though it was first introduced in 1994 at 30% (Tripp 2003).

One South African participant discussed the two types of quotas (reserved seats and party quotas), and argued that party quotas are preferable to reserved seats. *And there are so many different mechanisms. It depends on if you want an appointed parliament you can arbitrarily say we'll have so many women; or if you have reserved seats. But then you are making to me a fundamental problem. Are women the only ones who have to work on gender? (Interview with author, Johannesburg, 2014).* Her argument is that with the use of reserved seats the responsibility of addressing gender issues lies at the feet of those women elected through reserved seats. With a voluntary party quota it is the responsibility of the entire party, both women and men, to engage on issues of gender. Indeed, the type of quota could affect perceptions and the burden of responsibility. For example, sex specific quotas (e.g. reserved seats) run the risk of essentialising women as a special political group. However, while there is the danger that certain quotas, in this case reserved seats, could disproportionately burden women with representing gender issues, it is not an automatic result. *Like when we are dealing with women's issues, as I can say, yeah it's good because if you are a woman you understand your fellow woman, but it's not always about that. Women should be there to perform all their tasks, but not only for women, but also for the government (Interview with author, Kigali, 2013).*

In addition, those women that come in on reserved seats face stigmatisation with the perception that they have their positions on the basis of their gender and nothing else. Whereas other quotas (e.g. party quotas) are more gender-neutral by providing a minimum representation of both sexes (say 50/50), not just one gender (Krook 2008). Similarly, in the case of South Africa's ANC, when advocating for the quota women did experience stigmatisation by opponents. *I think one of the disturbing things that emerged at the time was the parity of women's empowerment...but it started to be challenged in 1991 at the ANC conference when we had to propose a policy for 30% participation in leadership positions of the ANC, how some of the male comrades ridiculed that proposition and ended up calling us "30%" (Interview with the author, Pretoria, 2013).* An interesting future study would be to examine current attitudes to quotas by individual men in the RPF and the ANC to determine what proportion of them are against quotas despite national and party policy. Similarly, it would be interesting to examine whether women have felt that they have been stigmatised as a result of quotas.

Another risk associated with reserved seats is that they may prevent women from winning seats outside of reserved seats – as non-reserved seats would be viewed as male seats given that women have their own special seats (Krook 2008). However, Rwanda is an example of a state that has avoided this by placing women on party candidate lists, and not only relegating them to reserved seats. In fact, it is this combination of reserved seats and simultaneously placing women on candidate lists that women politicians in Rwanda attribute their high representation level. *...The RPF decided that in doing their lists that they would do one-woman, one-man, one-woman, one-man. In other words, on the party list you'd be 50/50, equal, alright? And then the other parties then they took the cue and also implemented that, the other parties, so already there is the 30% women's seats, you know? And then women are coming on also on a party lists (Interview with author, Kigali, 2013).*

26

While with reserved seats there is the risk of only women having to address gender issues, on the other side of the coin is the case of party quotas; there is the risk of women being co-opted into the patriarchal culture and agenda in politics and government - though this is a danger no matter the type of quota (Krook 2008). This danger is because women may feel that they have earned their positions through their own merit and are not in their positions in order to represent women's interests. *And of course we'll have women that get there and we'll have the dangers of them being absorbed by patriarchy because they will consciously or unconsciously perpetuate the agenda; there will be what I usually call something like an honorary man and they will perform [that way] because they will then think 'I'm here in my own right' – which is true, some of them in the ANC...(Interview with author, Pretoria, 2014).*

Along the same lines, another criticism of quotas is the danger that women who reinforce the status quo would be elected, rather than women who bring any changes. Certainly, this concern is context specific because it is based on the assumption that a party or government has no political will to address gender inequalities. That being said, a consequence of electing/appointing women who reinforce the status quo would be women who are unqualified for the positions they attain - essentially token women (Krook 2008). Women politicians are not oblivious to this fact and those interviewed here have expressed opposition to such results. ... *Because where it becomes wrong is when they put women who are not capable. I also don't support that; you have a quota system for the sake of a female (Interview with author, Pretoria, 2014).* Those who advocate for quotas might argue that it is worth it to bring more women into decision-making power despite potential dangers. *...I am one of the people that has been a champion of quotas; I continue to be a champion of quotas and I'm aware of the dangers of quotas, but I'm also aware of the dangers of non-inclusion of women – and given the two I would rather go for the dangers of inclusion (Interview with author, Pretoria, February 2014).*

Indeed, this is not to say that there are no qualified women. *And if you don't have what you think are the very good women, you offer training for them, and it's usually not true that they are not there – because there is no political school that men, in the ANC for instance, go to especially for men for them to under-stand ANC...We go through together and some of them are even younger in terms of political understanding than the women that are there; but it is taken as natu-ral that a person who joins the ANC, a man who joins the ANC in 1994 is better than a woman who joined the ANC in 1980 (Interview with author, Pretoria, 2014).* This patriarchal attitude – that men are more qualified than women regard-less of actual experience, is overcome in this instance through the use of quotas.

In other words, in South Africa, the issue has not been whether or not women are sufficiently qualified, but has been to address the problem of having qualified women overlooked for the simple fact of their gender. *I'm a supporter, a great supporter of the quota system. I think that if you are treated in a society as a minority that has no power, that has no influence, that is marginalised as women are, we will not wait for a world that will not have patriarchy. It has been hundreds of years for women to prove to the world the fact that they can bring people into this world and nurture them and take care of them, they are capable. It has not happened. Patriarchy is beyond us. And I am not prepared that we wait until patriarchy disappears and that motherhood disappears, because there is subtle discrimination because you are a mother (Interview with author, Pretoria, 2014).* Indeed, there is a sense, from these women, that quotas are a necessity, and the argument should not be whether or not to have quotas, but how to ensure that they are effective.

Ultimately, the women interviewed here do not view quotas as an option, but a necessary instrument to redress structural gender inequality in politics. *My view is when as a movement, or any collective, you also look at a variety of instruments around which to reach your desired objective. So the quota for me is just but one instrument that women use world-wide to be able to assert, particularly where you change very chauvinistic bureaucracies that wouldn't naturally allow for women's participation (Interview with author, Pretoria, 2014).*

Interestingly, most of the women interviewed here did not receive their positions through legislative quotas (in the case of Rwanda). They include ambassadors, appointed executives, cabinet ministers, etc. With regards to Rwanda and South Africa, where women have come in on party candidate lists, it is also difficult to gauge which of those women would have been there with or without the use of quotas (this would require an in-depth investigation into the political party processes on making candidate lists)[4]. This raises two points. There is a commitment, particularly by the RPF and the ANC, to include women at all levels. It also indicates that women are not being selected as tokens, but as legitimate political actors. Both are encouraging in terms of addressing gender inequality in political decision-making. Not only do the levels of representation, but also the diverse positions that women hold in politics, suggest that in this specific area of politics, gender equality is becoming a reality.

---

[4] See Ballington (2007) who provides a party-by-party analysis of how candidate lists were finalised by several South African political parties contesting the 1994 national elections. All of the South African women interviewed here entered formal politics with the 1994 national elections.

In order to further understand the instruments that have resulted in Rwanda and South Africa's representation levels it is also important to look at the electoral system used and its relationship to the contentious quota.

Electoral Systems

Rwanda and South Africa both use the closed party-list proportional representation (PR) electoral system (Bauer & Britton 2006; ACE Electoral Knowledge Network 2015). The PR system is found to be the best system for increasing women's representation as it is found that it is used by most countries with high levels of women's representation (Britton 2008; Kunovich et al. 2007). The electoral system is not selected with a view to increase women's representation. Rather, it is selected because it enables minority representation (Britton 2008). An added benefit is that the system enables the implementation of quotas as candidates are not elected, rather political parties are elected. The political parties then place women on their candidate lists, rather than depending on the electorate to elect women candidates – thereby preventing patriarchal biases from affecting the election of women (Bauer & Britton 2006; Britton 2008). However, quotas and the electoral system alone are not enough to increase women's representation (Dahlerup & Freidenvall 2006). A political will is also a necessity. With the PR system the party determines which individuals are placed on the candidate lists, as well as the order in which they are placed (Britton 2008). In credit to both Rwanda and South Africa, it is exactly women's placement on the candidate lists that has played the most important role in increasing their representation. Women interviewed here credit the ruling parties in particular, the RPF and the ANC, for having favourably placed women candidate lists. ...*So, the RPF decided that in doing their lists that they would do one-woman, one-man, one-man, one-woman. In other words, on the party list you'd be 50/50, equal, alright? And then the other parties took the cue and also implemented that, so already there is the 30% women's seats, you know? And then women are coming on also on a party lists (Interview with author, Kigali, 2013).* In other words, it is the combination of the 30% reserved seats as well as the 50/50 national candidate list that has given Rwanda the highest representation of women in the world.

South Africa's ruling ANC has adopted a similar policy regarding their candidate list. *We have had a proportional representation system, so we started with the 30% and then today it is 50% [quota]. But we went much further than that;*

we said you can't then just put all the women at the bottom of the list, so it's got to be every third woman, every third member on your list has got to be a woman, or every fifth has got to be a woman... So we thought about the balloting system and used that kind of way to even out. Men didn't like it. It didn't matter because we had to put the political commitment of the organisation – if there's someone who didn't like it, too bad for them (Interview with the author, Johannesburg, 2014). It is important where women are placed on the candidate list as the party cannot win all the seats in parliament. Therefore, those highest on the candidate list would be the ones to win seats. If women are at the bottom of the list their chance of actually getting a seat is reduced (Britton 2008).

Perhaps it is this difference in candidate placements on the list that can explain the difference in representation for Rwanda and South Africa. As previously indicated, Rwanda has a representation level of 63.8% and South Africa has a representation level of 41.5%, a more than 20% difference. Whereas Rwanda's RPF has a 50/50 of women and men on its list, South Africa's ANC has at best every third candidate being a woman. In addition, the other major political parties in South Africa do not use quotas, further affecting how many women actually make it to parliament.

However, the picture is not dismal. The second largest party in South Africa, the Democratic Alliance (DA) has 30% women. The next party, the Economic Freedom Fighters (EFF), has 35% women. Interestingly a new party headed by a woman, Agang, won just two seats in parliament, of which none are women (Gender Links 2014). Had one been a woman, Agang would have achieved a 50/50 representation without the use of quotas.

In addition, South Africa's representation of women decreased in the last national elections in 2014, though by less than one percent, previously it was 42.3% (Inter-Parliamentary Union 2015). There are two factors attributed to this decrease. Firstly, the ANC won fewer seats than in previous years. Being the only party to have a quota, the decrease in their over-all seats would affect how many women they send to parliament (Gender Links 2014). Secondly, as previously discussed, women's placement on the candidate lists plays an important role. An examination of their 2014 candidate list shows that the top three candidates were men. Of the top ten candidates just 3 are women, and of the top 20 candidates just 7 are women (Independent Electoral Commission of South Africa 2014). In both cases women are less than 50%.

An examination of the entirety of the candidate lists for all parties that have won seats is outside the scope of this book. However, two important lessons can be taken. Firstly, women's representation in South Africa would be improved if all parties adopted and implemented quotas. Secondly, the ANC has to place women and men more equitably on its candidate lists. The same would apply to all other parties.

That being said, the central issue is not only about where women are placed on candidate lists to ensure an equitable representation. The issue of accountability and whether women representatives are tokens is not just an issue of quotas, but also an issue dependent on the type of electoral system. With the closed PR system the electorate votes for the party and not individual candidates (Kunovich et al. 2007). A result is that representatives are accountable to their party, not to the voters (though in a perfect world being accountable to the party would also mean being accountable to the constituents that elected the party), as previously discussed. However, a constituency system (such as a plurality-majority system) comes with its own problems. *...there are areas you spend so much money; you have what they call in Nigeria a 'Godfather'. In other words you are a candidate but everybody knows that you are funded by someone...then you have an agreement that when we appoint you we will get all the tenders (Interview with author, Pretoria, 2014).* In other words, in a constituency based system candidates can be funded by specific interests who seek to corruptly benefit on the election of that candidate. Therefore, a context specific electoral system could be devised. *One of the things you have no choice to do, we have to change our electoral system, and not go for constituency as the British do it. We coin our own constituency system (Interview with author, Pretoria, 2014).* A mixed system is a possibility, as other countries have done. 48% of the women in a 1999 IPU survey were elected under the proportional representation system, 39% under the majority system, and 13% under the mixed system. However, 64% believed that the proportional system is the best for electing women, while 17% said the majority system was most helpful for women, 26% said that a mixed system is best, and 7% said more than one system is best (Waring et al. 2000). It is interesting to note that while more women were elected in a majority system than a mixed system, more women were in favour of a mixed system than a majority system. It is outside the scope of this book to examine why this might be the case, but it is worthy of future investigation.

Mexico is an example of how a mixed system can increase women's legislative representation. Women's representation in Mexico most rapidly increased after a legislated national quota of 30% was introduced in 2002 (Hinjosa 2012). However, Mexico's mixed system comprises of single member district plurality and proportional representation. As per the author, in the 2006 national elections there was a significant difference in the amount of women elected for the single member plurality seats (15.3%) and in the proportional representation seats (36.5%) (Hinjosa 2012). This finding indicates that the distribution between the two systems is important, and the less proportional representation seats there are, the fewer women would be elected. Therefore, even in the case of mixed systems, a PR system is still necessary to ensure women's representation. The same finding has been made with studies done on New Zealand and the United States (Kunovich et al. 2007).

Conclusion

Considered together, Rwanda and South Africa are excellent case studies for the examination of instruments such as quotas and electoral systems on women's representation. They are examples of how political will by political parties is fundamentally important in PR systems to ensure that women are elected to leadership positions.

The interviews here also indicate that even those women who do not benefit from quotas are supporters of them. Most importantly, they believe in quotas despite the risks involved (such as co-optation and stigmatisation). Considered separately, Rwanda illustrates that more than one mechanism can be used to increase women's representation. While some scholars and activists might argue that women representatives are tools for regime legitimisation in Rwanda, this argument is overly simplistic (which is further discussed in the subsequent chapters). On the other hand, South Africa provides an example of what factors might cause a deterioration in women's representation after gains have already been made. This example should ideally open up a space to discuss ways in which women's representation can be protected, particularly in the case of voluntary party quotas where there are apparently no consequences for inconsistencies in women's representation. Perhaps a future study might poll South Africans as to how many would change (or keep the same) their vote if other parties were to adopt quotas and implement them consistently and equitably between genders.

Despite the overwhelming evidence that quotas and the PR system are critical for women's representation, these are not the only challenges that women leaders face, 'quota systems do not remove all barriers to women in politics, such as women's double burden, the gender imbalance of campaign financing, the many obstacles women meet when performing their job as elected politicians, and quotas may even contribute to the stigmatization of women politicians'(Britton 2008: 42). Some of the following chapters discuss amongst other things the relationship between representation and impact, the challenges that women face in their positions, and their double burden.

Chapter 2: Post-Conflict Representation and Impact

'So if you don't look at the need for change in this very holistic [way]... you can put any number of people in.'

The international women's movement advocated for 30% representation of women in national legislatures and positions of decision-making power. This 30% is called a 'critical mass' and is believed to be the important threshold at which women, collectively, would be able to represent women's interests (Powley 2006). Research has shown that this 30% critical mass has resulted in a change of political agenda to be more gender-sensitive (Fester 2007). In general, however, the impact of a critical mass is mixed (Kunovich et al. 2007). The increasing focus on the percentages of women's representation raises the following questions; Do women politicians necessarily represent the interests of women? Do women representatives mobilise together to promote women's interest legislation?

An example from the Rwandan context; Pauline Nyiramasuhuko (former Minister of Family Affairs and Women's Development), and Agnes Ntamabyaliro (former Minister of Justice) were all active perpetrators in the 1994 genocide (Hogg 2010). Interestingly, Nyiramasuhuko headed a ministry especially concerned with women's status, and yet participated in a genocide where women experienced brutal sexual violence. Similarly, Ntamabyaliro, as minister of justice, should not have been involved in genocide crimes and crimes against humanity. While these are extreme examples, they illustrate that we cannot assume that women are inherently peace-loving and good, or that they will be the protectors and saviours of the women that they represent. Indeed, some challenge the belief that all women share the same interests. This begs the question of how do you represent 'women' if they do not all share the same interests? This question leads to yet another; what are women's interests?

 ## What are women's interests?

Scholars describe women's interests in several ways; private sphere concerns related to gender relations, the gendered division of labour, a shared biology determines their interests, policies for the independence and betterment of women, issues related to gender gaps, and any issue related to the general society. Others believe that women's interests are those defined by women's movements around issues relating to women's every day experiences, while others argue that women's issues are entirely context specific, while others argue that women have a shared experience of oppression under patriarchy (Goetz 1998; Hassim 1999; Celis et al. 2008; Childs & Krook 2009). For all these many explanations it is problematic trying to examine a state's impact on women because it is difficult to define and determine what women's interests are at any one particular time. In addition, to explore women representatives is to assume that women's subjectivity is informed by their gender, and that gender is the main determinant of women's interests. While in abstract there may be women's interests that are universal, it is difficult to define them because there is no universal explanation for the causes of women's subordination as it is contextual and caused by many factors (Molyneux 1985).

Firstly, women's interests are extremely contentious because women have many other identities outside of their gender, such as race and class identities and experiences. These intersecting identities can cause different women to have conflicting interests. South African Ambassador and former MK commander, Thenjiwe Mtintso (2003) writes about the conflicting identities and experiences of South African women based on race and class, and that, for example, the assumption that a rich White woman and a poor Black woman would automatically have the same interests purely because they are from the same gender creates a false women's unity (Mtintso 2003).

That being said, Molyneux (1985) tries to categorise the various types of issues pertaining to women's interests (Molyneux 1985). She defines strategic gender interests that arise of out people's gendered social positions. She further argues that strategic gender interests are deduced from an analysis of women's oppression. Such interests would be the abolition of the gendered division of labour, institutional forms of gender discrimination, reducing the unequal burden of housework on women, and measures against gender-based violence, amongst others. Practical gender interests are those that concern women's day to day experiences within the division of labour as formulated by women who are having those experiences. These interests relate to immediate needs ad do not usually include strategic goals for women's emancipation (Molyneux 1985).

While there are many ways of defining women's interests, a great amount of literature discusses women's legislative impact in particular (which I discuss below). Based on this; a second fundamental issue is how do we define and measure impact? Is it representation levels in relation to legislative gains on women's issues, as much of the literature has explored? Are there any other ways in which we can determine the impact of women politicians? (Celis et al. 2008; Childs & Krook 2009; Goetz 1998).

Internationally, the findings have been diverse. In Latin America and Sweden women and men MPs have different legislative priorities. In the United States it has been found that women are likely to prioritise those bills that deal with social services, healthcare, women, family and children. Women are also more likely to initiate bills dealing with gender discrimination (Kunovich et al. 2007). African women MPs have different priorities from their colleagues in western countries. In Africa they are more interested in issues of land rights, HIV/AIDS, violence against women and sexual freedom (Devlin & Elgie 2008).

'To date, little scholarly attention has been devoted to the perspectives female political representatives themselves have about female political representation' (Coffé 2012: 286). Studies often theorise (e.g. Celis et al. 2008; Childs & Krook 2009) or look at legislative outcomes (Bratton 2005; Hassim 2006). This chapter examines the ways in which women politicians talk about impact; how they define it, what successes they have had, and what challenges they have experienced.

What is Representation?

Scholarly work on representation has had as one of its foundations the seminal work of Hanna Pitkin, *The Concept of Representation* (Pitkin 1967) . She finds that there are four main types of representation; formal, descriptive, symbolic and substantive. Formal representation is providing a person(s) authority to act on behalf of another. Descriptive representation describes the relationship between the representative and the represented in terms of characteristics. Symbolic representation simply refers to the perceptions and attitudes of the represented. Pitkin believes that substantive representation is the best of the four because here the representatives are reactive to the represented. In other words, the representatives must represent the interests of those that they represent, whether by being provided a clear and precise mandate or being given the authority to act on what they believe would be beneficial for the represented.

Newer literature on representation by Jane Mansbridge (2003), as discussed by Celis et al (2008), provides three other forms of representation. One of which is gyroscopic representation; the representative uses their common sense derived from their background and experiences. *I think that what we've gone through as women, once we are given an opportunity to be in decision making positions there is no way we can forget the needs that are there in our families, the needs that are there for women, the needs that are there for children, the needs that are*

36

there for having water nearby, the need for electricity, the need for good roads, the need for help, you know? We are not even saying that these are women who are going to deal with academic gender issues. These are women who are going to deal with practical gender day-issues (Interview with the author, Kigali, 2013).

The need for practical gender issues such as described above has been one of the reasons for having more women in leadership. Herndon & Randell (2013) have found that part of the rationale of having women in leadership in Rwanda is that women have different priorities to men; they are more concerned with issues of violence because of their suffering during conflict (as discussed in the Introduction Chapter), and because of the general discrimination that they have experienced as women (Herndon & Randell 2013). This belief was echoed by a South African. *One of the interesting things which I think is an experience for not just me, you'll find across the board for women parliamentarians and executives, is that particularly South Africa being a society post-conflict, we are very conscious about issues of exclusion and marginalisation and issues of women's empowerment – so all those came into there (Interview with the author, Pretoria, 2014).* As one participant explained it; the reasoning is not just to address issues of inequality, but to also improve the quality of women's lives. *But women ,because they know what it means for a household not to have water, for health service – that's why your socio-economic rights in my view are a very important chapter that I think participation of women in that negotiation process and in the Constituent Assembly for me I think were the gains that women made (Interview with the author, Pretoria, 2014).* In other words, a society could have gender equality, but in an undeveloped and inefficient state that would be an equality in poverty and lack of resources. What is needed is equality AND a better quality of life for everyone.

Institutional change is one way in which Rwandan and South African women politicians have had an impact. *What we did in South Africa is we changed the institution. Just as you have to change the shop floor if you want women to work – this is a fundamental thing, it's not enough to say bring women in because blacks come into business and they resign because the shop floor is organised for white males. So if you don't look at the need for change in this very holistic way or you don't understand it that way, you can put any number of people in (Interview with the author, Johannesburg, 2014).*

Similarly in Rwanda, women's progress has been linked to structural and institutional changes, which are believed to have entrenched women's gains. The belief is that not only have they altered the institutions, but also changed the political and social climate to make women's leadership and participation a normality rather than an oddity. Institutional changes include the 2003 constitution, the gender quota, and the ratification of regional and international protocols on women's participation (Uwineza & Pearson 2009).

Symbolic Representation – Have perceptions of women changed?

Symbolic representation is the broad social and cultural impact as a result of greater descriptive representation (Burnet 2011). The symbolic representation of women is partly precipitated by the belief that the increase in visible women in politics will encourage other women to become active in politics, whether it be engaging in political discussions or actively participating in politics in various ways. In Europe and the United States women are found to discuss politics more when there are increases in women's representation in national legislatures. Similarly, women also become more active in political activities. Significantly, the gender gap amongst adolescent boys and girls with regards to anticipated political activity ceases to exist once women's representation reaches approximately 33% (which is good news for proponents of critical mass theory). Essentially, there is a positive relationship between numbers and symbolic representation (Wilbrecht & Campbell 2007). Unfortunately, these findings reflect the situation in the United States and European countries. To the best of my knowledge, there is no similar comparative study examining Sub-Saharan Africa.

That being said, one of the biggest gains of women's leadership in Rwanda is believed to be the attitudinal and social changes that have resulted. *So, actually in Rwanda I would say that there is not that thinking that women cannot perform. You cannot perform on individual basis, but not generalising that women cannot perform... is no longer there. (Interview with the author, Kigali, 2013).* This attitudinal change regarding women's leadership has been attributed to women holding visible leadership positions. The important thing is that the change is not just about having visible women, but about women's work and impact being visible, thereby proving their competency, *Yes, because women got the chance to be in politics, we got affirmative action, the quota which is in our constitution... So we got that chance to enter the parliament, we entered other leadership positions, then that's when they arrived, 'oh, so these women can perform'. Because if you are not in leadership they cannot [see] whether you can manage to perform [or not]. But when you are there you are given responsibility and you perform accordingly, that's when the men, the whole population, started to realise 'ah!, so these women are able to perform' (Interview with the author, Kigali, 2013).* Similarly, Powley (2006) cites a Rwandan woman MP who argues that they should not be viewed as 'examples for examples' sake', but that their impact must be felt (Powley 2006: 18).

The need for symbolic hope is particularly striking and important for countries that have recently emerged from conflict. *When I was working for the ministry then I could see the women's lives changing; One; they had hope. You could see that even the one who was poor, the one who was sick, the widows, the returnees, they had hope. Then another thing that I saw with women was that they all wanted to work. Almost everybody wanted to participate (Interview with the author, Kigali, 2013).*

This is not to say that Rwandan women are fully empowered and that gender equality has been achieved in all sectors of society. Rather, there has been great progress over a short period of time. Coffé interviewed 14 women representatives in Rwanda, five of whom believe in symbolic representation (Coffé 2012). They believe that having more women in politics will encourage other women to enter politics, and positively impact women's perceptions of politics. *That 64% of parliamentarians would be talking women related issues, but there's something very important with the numbers, which is the symbolism and excitement that it gives, and the inspiration it gives other women. I've seen it. When parliamentarians were 52% then 56%, now 64%, and the reason they are becoming so many is because...women in the country are excited, I mean all the women are excited, they are thinking, 'I can go to parliament, I can do it.' (Interview with the author, Kigali, 2013).* Powley also found that women MPs feel that they are acting as role models, citing a parliamentarian who argues that the quality of life of future generations of women will be improved because they are being inspired to be ambitious (Powley 2006).

Burnet finds that the results of symbolic representation in Rwanda are far deeper than simply encouraging more women to participate in politics (Burnet 2008; Burnet 2011). As a result of increased descriptive representation Rwandan women feel they receive more respect in their communities, have gained more decision-making power in the home, are more able to speak in public forums, have gained greater access to education, and women have been encouraged to take on leading roles in other sectors of Rwandan society. However, significantly, the people that she interviewed attributed these changes not just to the visibility of women leaders, but the broad national commitment (driven by the RPF and the government) to advancing women. While women have been accepted as legitimate actors in politics and government, not just in politics 'women have found respect' (Burnet 2011: 320).

Despite their increased visibility in politics, however, in South Africa attitudes towards women's participation in society have not changed as significantly. Indeed, social narratives surrounding women leaders has framed them as threatening and emasculating, and they have been victims of ridicule, particularly the strong Black women leaders (Hassim 2006). *So for example and even today we have the numbers but you have the chairperson of the ANC Youth League saying the most misogynous things, anti-women statements (Interview with the author, Kigali, 2013).* Here the interviewee is indicating that when leadership within the ruling party, the party that has committed itself to attaining gender equality, makes anti-women statements it is difficult for society as a whole to take women leaders, and women, seriously and respect them and their contributions. Unfortunately, this particular example is not an isolated case.

There have been instances where a member of an opposition party has been ridiculed for her weight by a (male) member of the ruling party – ironically the party that has shown the greatest commitment to gender equity (News24 2013). Another example is a woman party leader's use of plastic surgery having made media headlines. In another instance a freedom fighter and minister was called a 'Barbie doll' by a male opposition member (Jordan 2014). And perhaps one of the most disturbing examples, due to the fact that it was woman-on-woman humiliation, was when a minister was ridiculed when a predominantly female union protested against her, using women's underwear as their protest emblem, in reference to the minister (News24 2013). In a provincial legislature, during proceedings a woman MEC was called a prostitute by a male ANC MEC as a point of order. The woman speaker agreed with him, and instructed the woman MEC to dress better in future (Davis 2015). What is striking is that these gendered assaults on women leaders, while only verbal, come from their colleagues (male and female). If those in the most senior positions in the country discriminate against, disrespect and humiliate their women colleagues, what chance for respect can an ordinary woman on the street hope to have? Indeed, such instances can be viewed as symbolic representation, but in a way that is detrimental to advancing women's status and treatment in society. In other words, the numbers mean nothing if it is not partnered with the right conduct by those men and women in leadership, in the media, in unions, etc.

Indeed, Geisler (2000) found that women experience criticisms by the media and the public as being directed more to their gender as leaders, than the work that they actually do. That being said, women within the parliament felt that over time men came to respect and value them more as legitimate members of the parliament (Geisler 2000). In addition, because the most visible female members of the parliament after the 1994 election, the Speaker and Deputy Speaker, were women of colour, this changed the perceptions about the demographic of parliament (Britton 2002a). *After I became Speaker, suddenly if you then look at southern Africa you found Speakers or deputy Speakers who were women in the provincial legislations, in the SADC region – because suddenly it was okay for women to be Speakers. You see, a lot of it is invitation and it encouraged women (Interview with the author, Kigali, 2013).* These findings vary from the 1990's when women MPs felt that parliament was still a white male institution and that competence was viewed as the domain of men and white men particularly (Britton 2002). As one interviewee put it, the symbolic representation of the first group of women in post-Apartheid South Africa may be one of the biggest ways in which they have changed society. *The second one is for the people to learn to deal with their prejudices against women. People can only deal with prejudice; they can only deal with attitude change if they have an experience. And so we were lucky that we could do our job well, which I'm sure even a man could have done, and people started to see that after all women can do it. And so to me I think for those of my generation that is then a contribution for others to say, 'women can do it, the women can do it'. (Interview with the author, Pretoria, 2014).* One woman interviewed expressed the belief that the average citizen's perspectives and prejudices about leadership have changed to accept the that women can be in leadership, also through women's appointments to the executive. *So visibly I think for me that statement of the first appointment of women ministers and deputy ministers in 1994 had more impact even changing the psyche of our society to come to terms with the reality of women's leadership and women capability (Interview with the author, Pretoria, 2014).*

Therefore, the women interviewed here feel that perceptions about women's leadership have changed, and yet they still experience attacks on themselves by virtue of their gender, and not on their competence or successes/failures as leaders. This indicates that some progress has been made in terms of changing people's ideas that leadership is a male domain, but women have not yet received the full respect of society, by both men and women.

In terms of tangible results arising from symbolic representation in South Africa; the voting gender gap in South Africa may have been affected by symbolic representation. In South Africa, 1.5 million more women than men voted in the 1999 national elections (Hassim 2006). Though, to the best of my knowledge, there is no study conducted to evaluate if this is a result of women's visible leadership. It may partly be attributed to the earlier workshops and sensitisation campaigns conducted for the 1994 election to ensure that women would not be prevented from voting by patriarchal or other obstacles. *And then we had all this money given to us by the European Union to do voter education. That became another activity – I don't know where we didn't go workshop – the rural women, this organisation, church women – we were everywhere again, exhausted day in and day out on voter education, encouraging women to vote... (Interview with the author, Pretoria, 2014).*

In Rwanda it is more difficult to ascertain the relationship between voting trends and women's representation as Burnet argues that voting is a requirement in practice as voting history is tracked on voter registration cards and national identity cards (Burnet 2011). Without a record of having voted, fines or exclusion from government services is a potential risk.

Changing people's set behaviours, mind-sets, and institutional cultures is one of the most difficult changes one can make in a society (Britton 2002a). Symbolic representation cannot be underestimated because it has far-reaching consequences. As indicated above, symbolic representation does far more than just change attitudes and beliefs. The changes to those attitudes and beliefs can result in visible and tangible changes to the ways that people live, resulting in substantive changes. Symbolic representation thus leads to substantive representation. For example, the first post-transitional women leaders in Rwanda had the effect of making more women shrug the idea that they could not be leaders by virtue of their gender. One interviewee expressed how it became more difficult contesting elections (for a reserved seat) as there were more candidates. *It's not easy. But the first one, 2003, that's after the transitional government, it was quite easy because I didn't have many competitors...So with that first parliament, 2003, we were many women because we were 47% that time. So what we did was to mobilise and empower women, more women. So for those 5 years we were there we had empowered very many, so they were enlightened, that's how even came many contesters. Like in my region, the first time we contested there were only 5, but in 2008 there were 28 women contesting for only 6 posts. So it was a struggle (Interview with the author, Kigali, 2013).*

This may be one explanation why Rwanda's representation levels are what they are today; women felt inspired to put themselves forward to take on leadership, despite having to compete against many other women, some of whom already had parliamentary experience. This shows a substantial shift in the mind-set of women about themselves and their capabilities.

Barnes and Buchard (2012) conducted a study on 20 African countries using data from 1999 to 2008 and found that as women's descriptive representation increased, so the political engagement gender gap decreases. This would be a form of substantive representation. To be specific, they consider the impact of women's descriptive and symbolic representation in national legislatures. That is;

does descriptive representation result in symbolic representation; thereby increasing women's political engagement in comparison to men. One of their findings is that if descriptive representation ranges between 25% and 35% - the gender gap between women and men's political engagement disappears. In this regard, the theory of a critical mass seems to hold true. This change occurs because women's representation is found to be directly correlated with women's attitudes towards politics.

In general, women are less likely than men to engage in all kinds of political behaviour and activities, which can be described as; talking about politics, interest in politics, contacting a member of parliament, contacting a party official, and attending a political demonstration (Barnes & Burchard 2012: 780). Interestingly, they also find that it is not enough to simply adopt gender quotas. What is important is that descriptive representation is seen i.e. that quotas are implemented. Also, women's low levels of political ambition partly stems from not having any political women role models (Kunovich et al. 2007).

Symbolic representation is crucial because for the laws to persist and be implemented they have to be supported by social values and norms (Uwineza & Pearson 2009). One woman described a changed social norm arising out of women's visible leadership. *First of all, we have worked as role model for younger girls. Now, formerly, if I had a boy and girl at home and I don't have little money I would educate a boy and leave the girl to marry, that was it. Primary she goes, or even she doesn't go to primary, that was it. But this time you have more girls in school (Interview with the author, Kigali, 2013).*

Substantive Representation for Strategic and Practical Gender Interests

With the sharp increase of women's representation in South Africa in 1994 women activists were excited about the possibility of being able to favourably influence legislation and policy for women and allocate more resources to women's interests (Hassim 2006). Similarly, Burnet argues that in Rwanda it is believed that if there are more women representatives, the society would be more peaceful and have gender equality (Burnet 2008). The literature exploring the substantive impact of women politicians in Rwanda and South Africa looks at the institutional and legislative impact that women leaders have had (e.g. Goetz 1998; Geisler 2000; Britton 2002a; Powley 2006; Burnet 2008).

Institutional Impact

It is not enough just to include women in institutions, it is also important to transform them (Fester 2007). In Rwanda's parliament women interviewed by Devlin & Elgie (2008) expressed feeling more comfortable and experiencing a pleasant working environment as a result of having more women present, as well as experiencing more respect from their male colleagues (Devlin & Elgie 2008). Women's strong participation is also visible; women stick to their convictions and are vocal in the debates (Elizabeth Powley 2006).

Similarly, in South Africa women interviewed by Geisler believed that men gradually began to become more respectful in their tone towards women (Geisler, 2000). In South Africa the changes are also more structural. ...*We set up a crèche but we found afterwards that women were not using it – that was their choice, but the staff were. We then stopped session by six o'clock so people could go home (Interview with the author, Johannesburg, 2014).* Britton (2002a) found that women in South Africa's parliament attributed the better working environment directly to the then Speaker – Frene Ginwala. The institutional transformation was not only directed at transforming it to accommodate women and men, staff members' working conditions were also improved. *So I went to Jay Naidoo who was then the minister of the RDP and I told him, I said, 'Jay, I have staff that are scared they are going to be fired because the Nats [the National Party] ran the campaign that when the ANC comes in they are going to fire all the Coloureds and bring Africans in; this is what they fought that election on.' So Jay said, 'What do you want?' I said, 'I want to make transformation, I want to change salary scales, I want to make all the staff permanent.' And I said, 'I don't even know how to read a parliamentary budget but I'll get the staff to do it but I want your agreement that you'll give me the money to do that.' And he agreed (Interview with the author, Johannesburg, 2014).*

The environment of the parliament was also transformed to make it a new, democratic people's parliament. *And the staff did gradually begin to understand about no tradition. They would come up and say, 'the tradition is ... or the precedent is ...' and I would say, 'not my tradition, not my precedent.' And one day a very, very clever man, on the rules he was tremendous and we used to lend him to the provinces to write rules and so on. But he knew the rules inside out, he was a stickler for precedence ...And one day he came to my office, I think about a year-and-a-half into the parliament and he said, 'Speaker, under the old regime we used to -.' I said, 'Kaspar, sorry, I didn't hear you, what did you say?' So he said, 'Under the old regime.' I made him repeat it again and he looked very puzzled. I said, 'Kaspar, welcome to the new South Africa.' I said, 'You know what you just said? You didn't use the word 'tradition', you didn't use the word 'precedence' – you told me about the old regime. Congratulations' (Interview with the author, Johannesburg, 2014).* Not only has the attitudes in and the workings of the South African parliament been transformed, but new institutions in the government and state have also been created.

The BPfA has called for the introduction of National Gender Machinery (NGM), and most governments have some form of NGM though there are mixed results in terms of implementation (Fester 2007; Kunovich et al. 2007). Besides transforming the institution of parliament, Rwanda and South Africa have both created new institutions to address gender inequality.[5] South Africa has the Joint Parliamentary Committee on Improvement of the Quality of Life and Status of Women (JMC), The Office on the Status of Women in the Presidency (OSW), and the Commission on Gender Equality (CGE) (Fester 2007; Anne Marie Goetz 1998). Despite the promising existence of these institutions, they are problematic. *Firstly, I critiqued the national gender machinery in South Africa very extensively. And even though Gouws, Siedman, Giesler all talk about the most advanced national gender machinery in the world: it is totally ineffective and I actually say that in my article as a gender commissioner (Interview with the author, Kigali, 2013).*

The CGE is an institution provided for by the South African constitution, and is intended to make the state responsible for gender equality rather than having it solely a women's problem. It is independent and intended to be rooted in the grassroots, every-day problems of South Africa's women, but it is funded by the state (Geisler 2000). An example of some of the challenges facing South Africa's NGM is under-funding and poor implementation of their recommendations, particularly of the CGE (Geisler et al. 2009). *You know Anne Seidman actually says, 'does the lack of finance for women's issues mask patriarchal intent?' That actually we set up a Gender Commission that has less funding than the Human Rights Commission. You have the gender commissioners that are paid at a deputy director level. You have the commissioners of Human Rights paid at a director level. You have a Human Rights Commission with a budget that's ten times of the Gender Commission – I mean, it is just set up for failure, not that money is everything but how do you actually balance out? How do you as a gender commissioner make recommendation to parliament and all the recommendations*

---

[5] See Mabandla (1994) for an analysis of the options in the early 1990's regarding what kinds of NGM would best suit South Africa. It is interesting to note that there was an awareness of the potential pitfalls of NGM, particularly of a Women's Ministry, that are evident today.

are somewhere up on the walls in some library, or they're very selectively taken?(Interview with the author, Kigali, 2013). However, the CGE is still relatively lucky compared to places such as Kenya where commissioners are unpaid (Fester 2007).

There is also the Department of Women, Children, and Persons with Disabilities, which is problematic in and of itself; *And you know how disastrous it was. I mean, how do you have one ministry with all the marginalised issues? It's just overwhelming. So she may be the best minister in the world but it's marginalised, like disability issues, youth issues, women's issues. So it's actually very, very sad (Interview with the author, Kigali, 2013).* Indeed, it is unrealistic and overwhelming to expect one department to have to address the needs of three different interest groups (never mind the huge challenge of trying to determine women's interests alone). Does this grouping of these marginalised people into one department reflect their status in society, and the real (lack of) commitment to address the issues and challenges that are unique to them, in the same way this has been said about the lack of funding? The effectiveness of the Ministry might be diluted by the sheer magnitude of the interest groups it has to serve.

In 2009, the African Development Bank (ADB) and African Development Fund (ADF) released a comprehensive report on South Africa's NGM. The report concluded that the NGM face numerous challenges outside of funding. These include lack of qualified staff, overlapping mandates, lack of authority to fulfil mandates, and lack of support. To address these challenges the report concludes that restructuring the machinery will not make a difference as long as the government does not have the will to ensure that these structures function effectively, are not given the necessary resources, and do not have qualified staff and leadership.[6] The picture is not bleak though. The JMC was the only official structure to have challenged former President Mbeki's government on the controversial arms deal, and it challenged the lack of provision of anti-retroviral drugs to rape survivors and pregnant women (Fester 2007).

The under-funding of NGM is also a problem in Rwanda. For example, The Ministry of Gender and Women in Development (MIGEPROF) has a 30 person staff, but only four deal with gender issues (two of whom are paid by the United Nations) and the remaining staff focus on children and family rights and policies (Debusscher & Ansoms 2013). The gender-focal points are often passed on to junior staff members who have no experience with gender issues (Debusscher & Ansoms 2013). MIDGEPROF is located in the Office of the Prime Minister and

---

[6] This report is an excellent resource as it examines the impact and challenges of all the gender machinery, at times providing provincial and municipal analysis as well.

gender mainstreams all national programmes and policies, and promotes women's social, economic and political empowerment (Uwineza & Pearson 2009). Some of the work of the Ministry has been to create a guarantee fund to enable women's access to credit. It also created the National Gender Policy, through consultations with various stakeholders, to ensure that gender concerns are addressed at all sectors of Rwandan society (Kantengwa 2010). The Ministry also founded Women's Councils after the genocide. It is from the Women's Councils that women are elected to the parliament's reserved seats. These Councils were established to mobilise and sensitise women on political participation for the improvement of their communities and country. The councils comprise of elected members from the national level down to the village level. They are also responsible for creating awareness of issues affecting women and following up on the BPfA. This system would be an effective way of ensuring that marginalised women (such as rural women) are elected to national bodies of decision-making and are thus able to represent those women who traditionally have no voice (Kantengwa 2010).

While MIGEPROF founded the Women's Councils it does not have a budget to service them and council members are unpaid. Activists in Rwanda state that the lack of funding is an indication of a lack of commitment, and that the councils are used more to transmit messages from the top to the bottom than anything else (Debusscher & Ansoms 2013). This is the same argument that has been used to describe a lack of commitment by South Africa's leadership, as discussed previously.

In 2004, the government of Rwanda adopted a National Gender Policy drafted by MIGEPROF. This policy is updated by strategic implementation plans every three years. The plan includes indicators for specific gender objectives and the responsible ministries are indicated. The Gender Monitoring Office is responsible for monitoring the indicators in the relation to national policies and programmes. Significantly, it does not monitor the public sector only. It also monitors civil society, religious organisations and the private sector (Debusscher & Ansoms 2013). This suggests that the lack of funding but the emphasis on meeting specific objectives is more an indication of a lack of available resources than a lack of commitment.

A final example is Rwanda's 2009 Executive Branch which comprised of 34% women cabinet ministers. Within this Executive Branch is the Gender Observatory which works as a gender ombudsman and which is charged with monitoring reforms and implementation. Male members of parliament supported and made recommendations on how to make it effective (Uwineza & Pearson 2009). It is believed in Rwanda that these institutional and structural advancements would serve to safeguard women's advancements in the event of a future change in the political will to have women's representation (Uwineza & Pearson 2009). Whether that is the case will remain to be seen in future years should Rwanda's leadership drastically change.

As discussed above, the allocation of resources to the NGM is an issue in Rwanda and South Africa. Gender responsive budgeting is one way in which resources can be allocated to women's interests, particularly poor women (Fester 2007). Both Rwanda and South Africa have had gender budget initiatives.

The Women's Budget Initiative (WBI) measures government budgeting and expenditure on women and tries to have departments become more gender sensitive in their financial planning (Anne Marie Goetz 1998). Unfortunately, the WBI ended once it stopped receiving donor funding from the Commonwealth (Fester 2007). In Rwanda, the gender budgeting office is in Ministry of Finance and Economic Affairs (Herndon & Randell 2013).

During the time in which these interviews were being conducted, Rwanda's Forum of Women Parliamentarians (FFRP) was working on mainstreaming gender budgeting. *One of our focuses of training is gender responsive budgeting. To make sure our planning and budgets are responding to the needs of men and women, addressing existing inequalities between men and women at the community level through the implementation of government programs. And after, at the end of training, people will say we have trained people. But the purpose of our training, the essence to which we are training members of parliament, members of FFRP? [It] is not to train them, it is to make sure they will vote budgets which are gender sensitive. And I will be prouder because law will have made gender budgeting compulsory in different government agencies...because before it was not monitored...and now it is going to be assessed (Interview with the author, Kigali, 2013).*

Rwandan Women MPs interviewed by Powley (2006) believe that having a woman chair the Budget Committee has been crucial in making the government budget gender-sensitive. Independent UN officials have also identified the chair, Constance Rwaka, as being effective at influencing the distribution of funds and the scrutiny of the budget. It was under Rwaka that gender budgeting was introduced and implemented in various institutions, including seminars on training staff and parliamentarians on gender budgeting (Devlin & Elgie 2008; Elizabeth Powley 2006).

Though the NGM machinery in Rwanda and South Africa has had variable success rates the good thing is that they are there. Going forward it is necessary to ensure that they are effective, but also that their recommendations are implemented and their work is not undermined. One idea to consider is that the failures of these institutions geared towards women are not necessarily the failures of women leaders, but the environment in which they work (for example, the lack of resources allocated to the NGMs). While outside of the scope of this book, it would be interesting to determine what role women ministers, commissioners, etc., together with the national governments, have had on the varying levels of success with NGMs.

Legislative Impact

An important example of the legislative impact both countries have experienced as a result of women's leadership is the equality clauses included in both constitutions. South African women, through the Women's National Coalition (WNC), were able to have the concept of a non-sexist South Africa included in the democratic constitution.[7] While women constitute a numerical majority group in the country they experience the marginalisation that is associated with being a minority group. Their rights are therefore protected under the constitution's Bill of Rights (Anne Marie Goetz 1998). *Actually one of the important clauses in that Constitution that in my view women fought for and achieved was the Equality Clause in our Constitution; both in the interim Constitution which was produced in 1993 and the final constitution in 1994. It [also included the] institution which is your Gender Commission, which I don't think if women didn't push for it would necessarily have been there. But also the Bill of Rights in terms of your socio-economic rights, I strongly believe that had it not been for women I'm not sure whether men seated would have really thought that we needed to think about rights or access to water.* Indeed, women's contributions to the constitution of South Africa were based on women's practical life experiences, rather than an abstract conceptualisation of women's rights (Mabandla 1994).

Similarly in Rwanda, women's civil society organisations made contributions towards the final constitution. One prominent women's movement leader, Judith Kanakuze was appointed to the Constitutional Commission, and ensured that many gender-sensitive clauses were included, such as the 30% quota requirement (Burnet 2008). The process of ensuring that Rwanda's constitution is gender-sensitive was a consultative one, which resulted in a women's memorandum that

---

[7] The WNC has been written about extensively, so is not elaborated on here. See Hassim (1999) Geisler (2000), Britton (2002), Goetz (1998).

was handed to the Constitutional Commission. The Rwanda constitution's inclusion of gender-sensitive clauses is partly influenced by CEDAW, as well as lessons gained from the South African experience (Kantengwa 2010).

Rwanda and South Africa are excellent case studies for women's political impact because of their successes, such as the constitutional success described above, also because of their representation successes. *Now we're at 50% - how many women we have, how many women ministers, even women of defence, even women minister of foreign affairs, energy – all these powerful positions by women – we have made it. But we were not vigilant as to how are we doing in terms of performing, and gender relations in society. You can have as many women ministers as you want but you will only end at that quantitative – but there is also the qualitative in that women are getting appointed to what would be the male position. However, you've got to also look at what policies we are churning out and how are we able, as the ANC and women in the ANC in particular, able to push transformation of gender relations or they'll begin to be back-stabbed because of the complacency, because of the victories that we are scoring (Interview with the author, Pretoria, 2014).* The same applies to Rwanda; is the quantitative representation (descriptive) being translated into qualitative representation (substantive), and is there a risk that women would become complacent over time as they have more successes and their numbers grow?

Studies on legislative impact in Rwanda and South Africa have been mixed, owing to different reasons. In both countries women have been instrumental in passing women's interests legislation such as the Inheritance Law in Rwanda. In South Africa there has been the Maintenance Act, the Domestic Violence Bill, and the Termination of Pregnancy Act, (Geisler et al. 2009; Goetz 1998). Also the Customary Marriages Act of 1998 which gave equal rights to customary marriage partners. It gives mostly rural women rights to their children on divorce and rights to inheritance and land (Fester 2007). Unfortunately it did not address issues of lobola (bride price) or polygamy (Geisler 2000). A former South African MP explained the inclusive and participatory process of how the act was conceptualised and drafted. *One of the things that they actually felt very strongly about was customary marriages and the perpetual oppression that women have who are married under customary marriage. So they approached the Centre for Applied Legal Studies at Wits University to look at that. And then we had the Joint Monitoring Committee on the Status of Women. And then we had the rural women, we had the women academics and we had the women politicians working together to write this Recognition of Customary Marriages Act (Interview with the author, Kigali, 2013).*

Another ground breaking piece of legislation passed in South Africa is the

Termination of Pregnancy Act. Abortion was first legalised in South Africa in 1975 but was only legally available in the case of rape, incest or risk to the mother's life. This resulted in as many as 400 000 back-street abortions annually, resulting in the unnecessary deaths of many women. In 1996 the Termination of Pregnancy Act legalised abortions on demand up to the thirteenth week, and longer if the foetus is abnormal, if the pregnancy is a result of rape, etc. (Britton 2002a).

Unfortunately, the legislature has not always been a place of success for women in the democratic South Africa. In 2014 The Ministry of Women, Children, and Persons with Disabilities sponsored the Women Empowerment and Gender Equality Bill in parliament. This bill was intended to over-ride all other such bills, and among its aims was to have women represented by 50% in all decision-making structures in government and private entities (such as private companies). Those entities that fail to comply would be fined 10% of their annual turnover and/or CEO's and directors would face a jail sentence. In March 2014 the bill was passed in a contentious session in which the opposition DA members left the parliament in protest to the bill. Complaints against it were numerous, including the argument (from the opposition and business leaders) that it was unrealistic to expect 50% women's representation. Many of those quoted in media reports against the bill included women leaders of opposition parties. The president of the Cape Chamber of Commerce, a woman, made the argument that women would naturally be drawn to some industries more than others (Citizen 2014; Ensor 2014a, 2014b). A few months after the bill was passed it was withdrawn by the Minister of Women in the Presidency, stating that there was insufficient consultation on the bill and that a new draft should be made with less emphasis on numbers and more on quality. By March 2015 there was no progress, and the bill had lapsed (Sabinet Law 2015). Regardless of the merits and failures of the bill, that it received wide-spread opposition, using patriarchal value-judgements as a basis, is indicative that attitudes towards women have not significantly changed. It also indicates that there is still widespread opposition to women's advancements and gender equality in South Africa's political and commercial sectors. This brings into question how much influence women leaders actually have when faced with opposition from powerful sectors. Indeed, that a woman from a NGM withdrew the bill suggests two things; the demands of the private sector take precedence over gender equality and/or that some women in NGM are not necessarily concerned with women's interests.

In Rwanda there was the Family Code of 1992 which made the husband the automatic head of the household, and in spousal conflicts over decisions the husband had the legal final say. Also the Commercial Code, which was first implemented during colonialism, required that women seek male permission in order to secure loans, credit, take legal action, to work or engage in economic activities (Schindler 2009). Since 1994 the RPF has a broad policy of protecting women's rights and increasing women's participation in the public sphere, and so does not restrict the work of women's organisations. An example was in 1999 when women's civil society organisations and women in government worked on The Inheritance Law (full name is The Law on Matrimonial Regimes, Liberalities and Successions). This law is famous for giving women the right to inherit property and land (previously only men could). This was an important achievement as after the genocide widows and girl orphans lost land and property to male relatives, which directly impacted on their livelihoods and survival. However, it is far-reaching in terms of women's empowerment and gender equality as it also gave women the right to enter into contracts, have paid employment, and open bank accounts etc. without the permission of male relatives. In practice women did have paid employment, businesses etc. but it was always subject to the abuse of male relatives because women did not have any rights to these (Burnet 2008; Kantengwa 2010; Powley 2006). The law on inheritance rights, while powerful in its conceptualisation and passing, faces the challenges of excluding poor women from access because their marriages were not formally registered (due to the costs involved), and as such they have no way to prove their co-ownership of land and property with their husbands (Schindler, 2009). Therefore, the legal ideal does not always translate into women's lived realities (Herndon & Randell 2013).

Rwanda also has the Gender-Based Violence bill which was introduced in 2006 and was the first substantive legislation to pass in Rwanda's post-transitional parliament (Uwineza & Pearson 2009). Like the Inheritance Law, it originated in the parliament, and not the executive, *So that GBV law, it was initiated within the parliament, Rwandan Women Parliamentarians Forum initiated it. You know most of the laws are normally initiated by the government and then they come to the parliament, we debate on them, and then they are passed like that. But that one was initiated within the parliament. When we initiated it of course the men were not for us, they didn't like it. Some of the provisions which we entered, they didn't like it because of penalties and all that, but later we really worked together and convinced them and they [supported] it (Interview with the author, Kigali, 2013)* This law makes polygamy illegal, defines rape, identifies different forms of GBV against women, children and men, and it provides guidelines for punishment for offenders. Significantly, men deputies were included from the beginning of trying to formulate the law, but some were opposed to banning polygamy and also the inclusion of marital rape as a crime. Nevertheless, it was through the contribution of women and men that the law has been passed (Devlin & Elgie 2008; Powley 2006). ...*So we used a comprehensive and holistic approach to gender-based violence, including psychological support, medical support, because if you don't provide medical support at the beginning you lose evidence for justice, so it includes psychological, medical, prosecution, and justice. And, initially for us it was an issue of sensitising people on gender-based violence, and helping people to realise that the survivors or victims of gender-based violence need more support than what we think. Because if a survivor is not helped at the beginning it will turn her to go to that culture of silence, not talking about what happened, because crimes of sexual and gender based violence; sometimes in African countries a survivor feels like, I would like to say a perpetrator (Interview with the author, Kigali, 2013).* One of Rwanda's achievements has been the decrease in reports of GBV. However, there is the criticism that a good GBV policy would actually result in more reports, not less (Debusscher & Ansoms 2013). Also, in 2013 there was just one women's shelter in Rwanda (Herndon & Randell 2013). In South Africa, as many as 5 women a week are killed by intimate partners and the reported rapes in South Africa are the highest of all Interpol members. Society is tolerant of gender-based violence and police are often hesitant to pursue such cases despite the Domestic Violence Act of 1998, which is viewed as one of the best laws for women in the world (Jewkes et al. 2002). Unfortunately, these harrowing figures of GBV in South Africa are seen to be a lack of awareness and a backlash against the progress that women have been making in society, *One, because we don't act strongly enough against it. The parties don't do much to educate their own members, which is where it should start. It is also a combination of two things in my view. One is if women move up, men feel they are moving down; they are used to being in authority, on the top. They resent women (Interview with the author, Johannesburg, 2014).* While GBV reports in Rwanda have been decreasing, in South Africa estimates are that only one in nine rapes are actually reported (Jewkes et al. 2010). Rwanda has restructured police services to train more personnel and recruit more women in response to GBV (Goetz et al. 2009). South Africa does not have a well-planned and implemented policy to combat GBV. The South African police has been reformed to address racial problems, but not gender problems; they are not sensitised with regards to gender issues. For example, an awareness campaign leaflet to address rape recommended that men not rape, but masturbate instead, wholly ignoring the real, social causes of rape (Graybill 2001). Perhaps the difference between Rwanda and South Africa's successes in incidents of GBV is the way that it has been handled in terms of policing, and not just the legislature.

However, Rwanda has not had a perfect legislative or policy track record in terms of women's interests. There was the passing of a labour law that actually reduced maternity leave. There is also little attention to those who become mothers through adoption or those not in heterosexual relationships (Herndon & Randell 2013). For example, in 2009 paid maternity leave in Rwanda in the formal private sector was reduced from twelve to six weeks. This was a measure implemented to attract more foreign investment into the country. The women's movement had tried to prevent this law from being passed, and it raised questions about the government's commitment to gender equality and the role of the women in the parliament (Debusscher & Ansoms 2013). That being said, Rwanda has since changed the maternity laws again. In 2015 the law was changed, giving women 12 weeks of paid maternity leave once again. The decision was made by President Kagame in a special cabinet meeting. The change is said to be a result of pressure from civil society and working parents. Previously, women would only be paid their full salary for the first half of their leave, and then lose 80% of it during the second half or return to work. Now the cost of the salary will be split in half between the employer and the government. The government's contribution will come out of 0.6% of the salary of every employee in the public and private sectors (Kwibuka 2015; News of Rwanda 2015).

Despite the earlier legislative gains in women's interests Rwandan women MPs interviewed by Devlin & Elgie (2008) explained that they are spending less time on gender issues as their numbers have increased. They have taken on other roles, and they feel that gender issues no longer have to be a personal issue since there are more of them. *Now, whether that number means that there will be more favourable decisions for women; I don't think it's necessarily true because at the end of the day these days there's very few gender specific legislations that we bring, we want to give equal opportunity to men and women (Interview with the author, Kigali, 2013).* It appears that Rwanda has decided to consider things more holistically rather than only look at women's interest legislation. *Another thing I will be more proud of is when we write the implementation of our economic development and poverty reduction strategy (which is still on-going)...because I take it as something that will bring many people out of poverty because our target is to go from 8.2 to 11.5, and if we achieve that target as a government, as a country, I will be sure many women have moved out of poverty because the big number of people in poverty are women. And also when the GDP will be able to move from 600 up to the target of the Vision 20:20 that will be a sign, a tangible sign for us to know that women have moved, many women have moved out of poverty (Interview with the author, Kigali, 2013).* In Rwanda there has been less time spent on gender issues in the parliament, which may indicate that they have become less interested in constituency work and gender interests (Devlin & Elgie

2008). Despite the legislative gains described here, Burnet writes that Rwanda has become authoritarian while trying to legitimise itself as a democratic state (Burnet 2008). She argues that because of this, despite the increases in women's representation, their power and influence has actually decreased. However, she argues that in the long run women's increased visibility and presence in institutions paves the way for substantive representation when Rwanda does become democratic. Secondly, women are gaining skills that would later serve them when they are able to have an impact. The problem with this argument is that it assumes that Rwanda's leadership is dominated by men and that there are no influential women. 'In the elections, RPF officials carefully selected candidates, and threatened or intimidated anyone else seeking office' (Burnet 2008: 365). What is lacking here is recognition that some of those officials might include women who are willing participants in the decision-making process. Secondly, those who are selected would then be loyalists who are also willing participants. Burnet's argument seeks to relegate even influential women to the victim category and it follows the essentialising ideology that all women are peace-seekers; if they exist in an authoritarian regime they couldn't possibly be supporters of it, but just victims.

Conclusion

It is difficult to ascertain what women's interests are as there are numerous definitions. However, if we consider some of the legislation that has been passed; such as GBV legislation in Rwanda and South Africa, the newest maternity leave laws in Rwanda, and the abortion laws in South Africa, I would argue that the legislatures in both countries have been concerned with practical gender interests, as defined by Molyneux (1985). In South Africa, the reform of the parliament could be a combination of practical and strategic gender interests. It concerned practical gender issues, such as having an accessible crèche for women MPs, but also reforming the culture of parliament to be more staff-friendly. Lastly, I would categorise the gender machinery as serving women's strategic interests as they do not service women's every-day practical requirements, in the way that, for example, abortion legislation would enable a woman to access abortion in the event of a rape.

Regardless of how we may classify the kinds of interests, the institutional and legislative reforms that have occurred in Rwanda and South Africa since 1994 have been mixed. Ground-breaking women's rights' legislation have been passed but the NGMs are under-resourced. While Rwanda and South Africa have surpassed the critical mass figure of 30%, they are examples that there is no guarantee that having descriptive representation will automatically result in a substantive representation. Similarly, symbolic representation has had mixed results as well. Rwandan women have gained more respect as women in their society, while South African women leaders are continuously attacked on the basis of their gender by various sectors of society. The examples discussed here indicate that social, economic and political pressures may play a far greater role on women's rights than the numbers of women representatives.

Chapter 3: Impact: Strategies, Accountability and Challenges

'I don't know how I can explain it, but I think the challenge is to play politics positively.'

The idea of women's representation comes with the assumption that there would be a specific group that would be held accountable for a mandate and programme (Mtintso, 2003). Women may have access and be able to participate, but the issue becomes one of the impact of such a presence on all sectors of society. Rwanda and South Africa have mixed results in terms of symbolic, institutional and legislative outcomes, as discussed in the previous chapter, *But it cannot end there; quantity is important but so is quality. So quantity is towards the creation of qualitative transformation. So I have…what I called access, participation, transformation – and these go together – so you don't have just access (Interview with the author, Pretoria, 2014).* In the previous chapter I discussed some of Rwanda and South Africa's legislative and institutional successes and losses for women's and gender interests. Transformation has been achieved but there is still room for improvement, such as the better allocation of resources. Creating NGM, reforming institutions, and changing the laws does not guarantee justice and equality for women (Goetz et al. 2009). Social structures also have to be reformed for women to be fully emancipated (Britton 2002a).

As indicated in the previous chapter, an overwhelming amount of literature looking at women in politics has looked at the symbolic and substantive (institutional and legislative impact) representation of Rwanda and South Africa resulting from their descriptive representation. In this chapter I explore other types of changes and transformations that women have made, the ways in which they have done so, and what challenges persist.

Grappling with Culture

One of the obstacles to gender equality is the role of culture. Particularly in the private sphere it is difficult for women to exercise their rights when faced with traditional and cultural obstacles (Fester 2007). Culture can also affect women's representation and participation at various levels. Research has shown that attitudes about women and politics can predict women's representation across countries (Kunovich et al. 2007). In Rwanda and South Africa, culture has been used to bolster women's arguments for their participation in politics. In South Africa, however, the issue of culture in politics has been more contentious.

Politicians, especially women politicians, in Rwanda use culture and tradition as arguments for certain reforms. They push these through as a revival of pre-colonial Rwandan tradition (Uwineza & Pearson 2009). Rwandan politicians use the image and role of women as mothers in order to bring about social change. At first glance, this appears to be an essentialist construct. However, it is a deliberate strategy that is being used to create a peaceful symbol and image of women to facilitate radical reform (Herndon & Randell 2013). Interestingly, women MPs have also challenged cultural practices, such as polygamy, that oppress women. At the same time they have used other cultural practices to fight for reform and legislation that is in women's interests (Uwineza & Pearson 2009).

Traditionally, Rwandan women were peacemakers, preventing men from waging war by influencing their husbands, fathers, and sons etc. They did so by removing the strings tied around their waists and placed them in the way of the man. It was believed that if a man crossed over the string, he would die in battle. As a result, men were dissuaded from going to war. It is this role of peacemaker that is now used as a link to women's present role as rebuilders of Rwanda, and propagating the belief that having more women in leadership will result in a more peaceful society (Uwineza & Pearson 2009).

Powley cites parliamentarians discussing the impact of women on children's interest legislation; arguing that women are in a better position than men to know the needs and challenges of children because men are removed from care-taking (Powley 2006). Similarly, when lobbying men on women's interests, women MPs frame the discourse around mothers and daughters, not wives. The women explain the impact of the legislation on mothers and daughters because men are less likely to feel threatened when it is not framed as an attack on them as husbands. In this way it is also personalised, and not framed as an abstract rhetorical issue (Powley 2006). *For us there is no way we force things. What we do; we lobby. We lobby our fellow men, we discuss, you convince…That's how we do it. When you try to force and use strength, a woman to a man, you're worsening the whole thing and I think that's why some parliaments are failing to get a good number of women in the parliament, because they want to force their way, so for us that will not work within Rwanda. You lobby, you discuss, you do this and that and later they come to accept. And even to add on that, you have the political will of the government, his Excellency the President of the Republic. He is really for gender issues (Interview with the author, Kigali, 2013).*

Around the world, historical discourses and narrative shape national identity. Rwanda has chosen to use tradition where it is conducive to improving women's lives (Uwineza & Pearson 2009). Rwandan women's contribution to rebuilding the country in the aftermath of the genocide is a part of the public narrative of Rwanda today. Government officials are a part of this discourse, including President Kagame who calls not only on women, but also on gender sensitive men, to protect women's interests (Elizabeth Powley 2006). It remains to be seen whether this image and symbol of the Rwandan sister and mother, and nurturer, will change or continue to be useful, or eventually even restrict women (Herndon & Randell 2013).

In South Africa women began their activism on the basis of their status as mothers. Motherhood was what united women across races, classes, and rural/urban divides. However, this motherhood essentialism also propagated their continued subordination under the broader freedom movement (Geisler 2000). This interviewee explains that not enough has been done to address how culture affects women; *we have as society and as the ANC not worked very hard on the understanding of culture. We use it conveniently. When it's convenient for us culture is static and it's not dynamic, it does not change. When it's convenient, culture is dynamic and it changes.* She went on to provide an example of how culture is still being used, incorrectly even, to oppress women, *You find young men now having many girlfriends and I know in Orlando, I was doing some little research there and they said, 'I want to have five wives finally. But I cannot have five wives if I don't start checking them out.' So now they are checking them out and that's a misrepresentation of the culture. And then you have these weddings where a man just takes five at the same time and they all smile there. That's not what's done culturally before. So it's a misrepresentation of our culture and that then puts back some of the gains that we have made (Interview with the author, Pretoria, 2014).* In other words, while Rwandan women leaders have successfully appropriated aspects of their culture to bolster their position, they have also interrogated those practices that oppress them. In South Africa culture has not yet been engaged with sufficiently at the leadership level. There are exceptions, as I cited the example of the customary marriages act in the previous chapter, which protects women who are in traditional marriages. South Africa's constitution protects people's rights to practice their culture, as long as those practices do not impinge on the Bill of Rights, which promises a non-sexist South Africa (Constitution, 1996).

In South Africa women's struggles have centred on the practical needs of women (or practical gender interests) (Mtintso 2003).[8] *For example, in the 1999 elections the Democratic Party, Tony Leon, used to go on and on and on about the ANC has not improved the life of South Africans, there's no change, and so on. So I was in parliament, I had welcomed the women, I think it was the 2 million households that had been given running water, so I invited them to parliament. When we came into power there were, I think, 10 - 12 million households without running water. And the millions, it's when the million households were given water that we brought them to parliament (Interview with the author, Johannesburg, 2014).*

Another woman talked about the provision of social services that have been provided by the ANC government, *there has been a change of the social services...they benefit women, whether it's access to water, to electricity because they're the ones who would have been fetching water. So it's not exactly true to then say that the Constitution has not been translated into reality. It is true that there's still a lot to be done (Interview with the author, Pretoria, 2014).* Indeed, South Africa has reformed the social welfare system to include the needs of Black and Coloured women, who are the most impoverished populations in South Africa (Anne Marie Goetz, 1998). It has also ensured that rural women have been represented in parliament, *we had persuaded Ma Lydia Kompe, she was the head of the Rural Women's Movement, we had insisted we wanted her in parliament and put her on the list. 'I said, 'Yes, you; who's going to speak for rural women if not you.' And I think it must have been the second year or something when the National Party people were heckling her. So she was on the podium speaking and she just turned around to them and said, 'You keep quiet, I'm dealing with all of you later on.' I could have stood up and cheered (Interview with the author, Johannesburg, 2014).* There is a huge significance in this moment. This was a leader for rural women, leading in an institution that had denied them not only their participation, but consistently passed laws that delegated them to second class citizenship in the country of their birth. In fact, they were third class citizens owing to their dual oppression as both Black people and women. The symbolism of that moment is enormous; especially because those heckling her were members of the party that formed the Apartheid government.

In some cases religious institutions have been reformed as well, *And then there was a ruling in the South African Council of Churches (SACC) that no one should be the general secretary if you are not ordained; so that disqualified me,*

---

[8] Ginwala (2001)has written about the mass, and sometimes militant, mobilisations of South African women in the early 1900's, as well as women's exclusion and the entry into the then South African Native National Congress, later the African National Congress.

but I didn't want also at that time to be the general secretary of the SACC because there were so many opportunities now for black people, black women, and I thought with my experience I have so many offers. And lo and behold they thought, no, they wanted me to have the South African Council of Churches and so one of the wonderful things they did, my church and others, was that they had to change their Constitution so that I could be able to take the job. So I often say I made a break for women (Interview with the author, Pretoria, 2014). This is not to say that religious institutions in South Africa have been reformed to have more gender equality; rather that there are women who are breaking the proverbial glass-ceiling in masculine dominated professions. They are shattering the professional limits that were set for women.

Accountability & Implementation

Along the same theme of culture; Rwanda has created a unique accountability system known as Imihigo as a means of improving development and local government reform. It is an old tradition in the country, but has recently been revived to meet the modern challenges that the country faces. In this system two parties sign a contract committing to attaining a specified goal. Failure to do so leads to dishonour within the society. The initiative was led by the Rwanda Ministry for Local Administration (MINALOC) and the Ministry of Finance and Economic Planning. Targets are informed by the development objectives of the country such as Vision 2020, and the Millennium Development Goals (MDGs). Kagame is included in the contracts and signs them with district leaders, and his requirement to is make the necessary resources available to meet specified goals. Other participants are at the sector, cell, village and household levels. The contracts include information on targets, performance indicators and resources available. Evaluations are done three times annually by officials from MINALOC, the Prime Minister and President's offices. Significantly, GBV has been included as a standard by which district leaders are evaluated in the household surveys. This is an example of the country's commitment to addressing gender issues (Goetz et al. 2009; Ngendahimana 2012). *The performance contract is in every organisation, even in every ministry, there is that program. And the minister signs it with his staff, his department heads, 'I'm going to do this and that and if you don't perform you stay away', that's how it is. It started from his Excellency [President Kagame] and the district, then went to the ministry, went to parastatals, went into other government organisations (Interview with the author, Kigali, 2013).*

What is interesting about the Imihigo is that this system not only holds government accountable, but also the family and households for Rwanda's development and well-being, *It started at the national level, now it is in the family. So, 'what will we do, what are you going to do, what are you achieving, what are your goals? What are you going to do for the family?' If development is there to be achieved it starts from the home. Why can't we also do it in the home? But doing it local leaders must be there, they have a general meeting at the village level, each family starts talking, 'me, this year I'm proposing to do this and that'. And they have a small book where they record it. And even the local authorities have their copy of the contract performance for his family, you see? So we have our own initiatives, local initiatives so that people can work... (Interview with the author, Kigali, 2013).*

The Rwanda Governance Board itself has said that as yet not enough research has been done to explore the impact of the Imihigo (Rwanda Governance Board 2014). That being said, reports indicate that recent years have seen districts scoring high success rates in their evaluations with improvements in health and educational infrastructure, and access to water and electricity (Ngendahimana 2012). Media reports have also indicated that numerous leaders have resigned over the poor performance of their districts in the Imihigo, or their failure to meet targets. The pressure to perform is evident by the resignation of one leader who scored an 80% success rate, but whose performance was still low in the over-all rankings of the districts (Musoni 2015). However, there are no penalties at the household level, *there is no one who forces you, whether you are going to do it or not, nobody penalises you for that like at the government levels. Those ones are penalised if they don't perform, some with their jobs. At the family level it is just teaching you how to plan, how to do things. Some say, 'I am going to buy a piece of land, I think this year I don't have a piece of land, maybe I will buy it, I will work for money to buy it (Interview with the author, Kigali, 2013).* Imihigo is an example of how context-specific accountability systems can be created, particularly in a PR system where candidates are mostly accountable to their parties.

The Women Empowerment and Gender Equity Bill (which I discussed in a previous chapter), is an example of how the South African government has tried to implement a policy for accountability for women's interests, particularly in the private sector. This legislation would have enabled the government to fine or prosecute public companies that do not include women in senior positions. The public sector pushed back against this, and the bill which had already been passed, was withdrawn for further consultation, but eventually lapsed (Ensor 2014b; The Citizen 2014). This example indicates that there is a will to have some kind of accountability for women but that will can be superseded by other interests, such as business and economic interests. In other words, women can't expect the public sector to answer to them, nor can they rely on the government to advance their interests where there are other competing interests.

In the way that district leaders are accountable for GBV objectives in the Imihigo system, accountability to women means that institutions have to enable processes whereby women can hold decision-makers accountable for their actions. Perhaps the Women Empowerment and Gender Equity Bill failed because ordinary women have not held the parliament and government accountable for not pushing hard enough for women's interests. Commitments to women can only be met if there are systems in place to hold stakeholders accountable (Goetz et al 2009). The Progress of The World's Women 2008/2009 United Nations Development Fund for Women report asks the question, 'who answers to women?' (Goetz et al 2009: 1). The report looks at five sectors; politics, services, markets, justice, and aid and security. It looks at the success and challenges that women have had in finding and resolving gaps in accountability. Accountability is defined as including 'assessment of the adequacy of performance, and the imposition of a corrective action or remedy in cases of performance failure' (Goetz et al 2009: 2). In the cases of Rwanda and South Africa, having gender-sensitive constitutions, NGM, gender-sensitive institutions, and women's interest legislations; the issues now become ones of implementation and accountability. The true mark of accountability, as Goetz et al argue, is if policies and laws are actually implemented and positively impact women's lives, which has been the biggest challenge (Goetz et al. 2009). *As I say...gender neutrality in policy legislation does not equal change; it's in the application and that's where you have to put the details and have an appreciation (Interview with the author, Pretoria, 2014).*

To create accountability to women, women should be able to participate in debates, delegations and performance assessments. The standard by which decision-makers must be held accountable must include gender equality as an indicator. The key is that those in power must be held accountable to women. To improve accountability there needs to be multi-party women's caucuses, parliament committees for gender issues, political will from the ruling party, and government departments working together (Goetz et al. 2009).

To improve accountability to women reform at three sites has to happen; the normative, procedural and cultural levels. Normative means that the institution has to be reformed to answer to women. The procedural level includes changes to incentives so that there are rewards and repercussions for performance. The procedural level also includes reforms to performance measures and reviews to include performance on gender-sensitive targets. The cultural reform refers to changing attitudes in both public and private institutions, which is a more long-term project (Goetz et al. 2009). As discussed in the previous chapter, symbolic representation is one way to have cultural reform, and has had mixed results in Rwanda and South Africa. Also discussed in the previous chapter, normative reform has occurred in both countries. While the previous chapter also partly dealt with the procedural reform (such as gender machinery), this chapter explores issues of accountability and monitoring women's progress.

As discussed in the first chapter on Proportional Representation Electoral systems; Rwanda and South Africa's electoral system holds elected leaders accountable to party leaders and not the voters. In addition, one of the inherent problems of elected systems is that they hold more powerful individuals and entities accountable to less powerful actors (Goetz et al. 2009). In South Africa more women than men vote by approximately 1.5 million (Hassim 2006). This means that women's votes matter immensely; they can deny their vote to parties that have not shown a commitment to gender equality and improving the conditions of women's lives. Goetz et al (2009) argue that women should form broad-based coalitions whereby voting constituencies can demand that politicians are accountable to them. That being said, it is a difficult situation in real terms because there is only one political party (the ANC) that has shown a commitment to women. *Patricia de Lille started a political party, the ID...I still was a very central ANC member but I as a feminist immediately phoned and said, 'Look, I'm interested to understand what your policies are.' And they couldn't give me any policies; they had no policies on women. So the ANC still have the best policy. The point is when are they going to start internalising those policies? (Interview with the author, Kigali, 2013).* While this interviewee describes the lack of alternatives in political parties in terms of policies for women, she also highlights something important. That is, this party was founded by a woman but had no policy with regards to women, indicating that having women's senior-most leadership would not be a guarantee for representation or implementation.

In the same way that South African women could form a powerful voting bloc, previously I discussed how Rwandan women use a gentle approach of lobbying men to pass legislation in favour of women, it does not mean that they are not aware of the power that they have as a collective; *I was at a conference in Nairobi three weeks ago. Talking about making quotas for women...making them work. And the Kenyans were saying, 'Rwanda you've made so much progress, what is your secret, share with us?' I say there is no secret. The only thing I can say is work; start with your parties, start from within your parties. You are the majority; you are the ones who put these men in power, right? Yes. So claim your [power] right from your party. Can you imagine which party would survive if all the women would [do that]....? (Interview with the author, Kigali, 2013).*

In terms of looking at women's political power, Hassim has already made the argument that we should look at women's political participation outside of electoral voting, such as protest actions, submissions to parliament and strikes as this is where women have historically been active in politics, and these are ways in which they exercise their rights as citizens (Hassim 1999). We also have to look at women's power and influence on policy within political parties, which has hardly been done in Africa (Hassim 1999 2006). In Brazil women politicians express that the same patterns that happen in the private sphere have developed in the political parties. Men make the decisions and women perform the practical tasks (Goetz et al. 2009). Learning how much influence women have on party policy, decisions, programmes, election campaigns, etc. would perhaps help us to understand if and how women's roles in the party translate into government. I would also argue that within that, we need to examine the power and influence of women within the executive branch of politics (both party executives and cabinet).

The Executive

Some research has already been done on women and the executive (Adler 1996; Bauer 2011). Believed to be one of the strongest NGMs is Chile's National Office for Women's Affairs (SERNAM). It is believed that part of its strengths is its leadership in the form of its director, who also holds the position of Minister of State and so is a participant in cabinet, thereby able to influence policy in the executive, indicating the potential influence that executive women have over policy to benefit women (Goetz et al. 2009). In South Africa women have been well represented in the executive as both ministers and deputy ministers, and in social welfare and perceived masculine ministries such as foreign affairs and trade and industry (Waring et al. 2000). Rwanda has also appointed many women to cabinet. Approximately two-thirds of members of cabinet are women (Debusscher & Ansoms 2013).

Unfortunately, women in the executive express feeling isolated and lonely because they have to represent the majority as a minority (Waring et al. 2000). A

South African former cabinet member expressed feeling lonely in her position, *Secondly, in the workplace – you know, one of the things that at times we talk little about as women leaders is the isolation of office – one, because there are still stereotypes in societies that go along with women's positioning in positions of power. It's not regarded that you could have gone there out of merit: it's either you have gone there out of affirmative action or you have gone that process, led your way through. So before people accept your leadership they'll still be thinking 'We wonder how she got there?' (Interview with the author, Pretoria, 2014)*. This feeling is corroborated by a cabinet member from the Pacific Region,

It is very evident that while women are in the minority in cabinet, and the doctrine of ministerial collective responsibility applies, the women who battle for women in the secrecy of cabinet will be forced to comply with the male majority and can never defy that beyond cabinet without fear of being forced to resign. This is a distinctly unhealthy situation for women, and any representatives of minorities (Waring 2000: 123).

Though not a solution to the problem of how to ensure that women are able to influence the executive, this interviewee and her colleagues found a solution to the isolation that they experienced. *So what happened was that when we started in 1994... a group of women volunteered themselves to give us a platform once a month on a Saturday where we could sit and talk about our own experiences and they'll be there with strategies, this is what you can do, and so on. And these were young women who were leaders in their own space in the corporate world, in civil society, but who were willing to give just their time for your to vent and cry if you needed to cry – but is for me a very important tool because we knew that if things were to happen could pick up the phone and say, 'I think there is an issue here' (Interview with the author, Pretoria, 2014)*.

What is interesting in terms of the South African cabinet member experiencing a sense of isolation is that she worked in a cabinet in which women were not a minority. Could this be an indication, again, that numbers are not as effective as the international women's movement had hoped for? Future research into women and politics in Rwanda and South Africa should consider the role and influence that executive women have in party politics and in the cabinet.

New Ways of Exploring Substantive Impact

In understanding the power and influence of women in the executive branch of government there would need to be an examination of whether their numbers make a difference, but also it would indicate, for example, whether women executives attempt to, and succeed in advancing gender/women's interests within their own ministries as well.

Childs and Krook argue for the examination of critical actors as a better way of exploring impact because it opens up new ways of thinking about impact and removes the assumption that only women, and a large group of women, can represent women's interests. (Childs & Krook 2009). Other scholars and practitioners have also made the argument to shift away from the numbers game and begin focusing more on substantive representation (Fester 2007). However, there are difficulties here as women are not the only constituency to require representation and representatives are not always able to act as individuals, *It's difficult to make an assessment of them as women because parliament is not an individual thing; parliament is a collective where you have a group of people called parliamentarians. I don't know; I've never been in parliament myself. I've gone there to report to my bosses, parliamentarians, and the women have asked me questions in parliament that are difficult, as males do, and they have made contributions to discussions. [In] my own experience of 14 years I was accountable to a committee...and the woman who sat in our committee [for] the 14 years was sharp as a knife on budget. And she would always ask the most precise questions on budget; she understood budget more than the males. So it is difficult to assess them as a separate group because they belong to different parties and they work as a collective – so where you to assess her as a woman because the caucus group decides on who speaks. And I don't think that they decide on who speaks because you are a woman...(Interview with the author, Pretoria, 2014).*

In addition, it is also difficult to draw conclusive links between women and policy results because of the other factors involved in the process of creating to adopting policy. Sometimes, international standards and forces make individual legislators powerless (Goetz 1998). Especially amongst liberal or left-leaning governments it is hard to tell if a woman is voting for women's interests because she is a woman concerned with women's issues, or if she is following the liberal party line; making it complicated to assess women's impact in some contexts (Kunovich et al. 2007). However, it is worth exploring possible ways of looking at how individuals (men and women) are able to influence all sectors of government for women and gender issues.

Developing Childs & Krook's idea further, Celis et al believe that not only should we look at critical actors, but we should also consider different sites of representation and the circumstances within which representation occurs (Celis et al. 2008; Childs & Krook 2009). They argue that we should ask the questions; who, how, why and where? Part of the problem of previous research, they argue, is that it focuses on women in national legislatures. We should open the scope of analysis to include party members, members of civil society, ministers, bureaucrats and legislators (Celis et al. 2008). Not only this, we should also examine the conditions within which they emerge, and the sites at which an impact is made. For example, literature has explored the relationship between NGM and the women's movement to determine if the former is reflective of the demands of the latter (Celis et al. 2008).

In this book I have made an attempt to not over-emphasise women parliamentarians, but to explore the ways that other women political leaders may (or may not have) had an impact. The interviewees here come from different levels and institutions of government, including ministers, parliamentarians, ambassadors and executives. Below I explore some of the ways an impact has been made outside of institutional and legislative reform.

Other Kinds of Substantive Impact

In keeping with the theme of critical actors, we should explore individual women in diverse positions. *We have a woman who is the head of the environmental authority here, which means that even within the environmental regulations and legislation that are being passed there are laws that have a gender perspective. So really the presence has a lot of impact. People may not see it, but it has a lot of impact. Because when people are debating things in parliament, for example, if it really really affects women, because women parliamentarians, they know from their own experience, they know from their own homes, and so on and so forth. So to me, why has nobody ever questioned the quality of men? Or the impact of their presence? (Interview with the author, Kigali, 2013).*

For example, at the local level it has been found that having more women in the civil service means better governance on women's interests. In a study conducted in India it was found that women at the local level were more likely to make complaints and/or requests on things such as water resources. It was also found that more drinking water projects were initiated by female-led councils. In areas where more road building jobs went to women, women led councils implemented more road projects. Similarly, in Norway it was found that there was a direct relationship between childcare coverage and women-led city councils (Goetz et al. 2009).

Another example is a woman who holds an executive position within a government department concerned with the economy and development, *Or when I move around and I see a new hotel, a new project, a new bank that we facilitated coming into the economy it is very motivating because you see the results. For example, times I've gone to a bank that we've worked with in coming to the country, enter the bank and I see all these people working and then I see that all these hundreds of people got a job because this investor come and these are probably supporting the wives, the family, the whatever, and so the people that are actually benefiting from all of this are about 500 and I'm like, 'oh my god this is important!' That is very motivating (Interview with the author, Kigali, 2013).* In other words, sometimes a leadership success may or may not directly impact women, but that success cannot be discounted in interrogating women's leadership impact.

The demanding roles of ambassadors or those who work in the diplomatic core would also be a way of developing new knowledge about women and politics, for example, *I think in most of the things that I've done it's one of the most fulfilling for me to be able to go outside and represent my country. And it's a highly responsible area because when you are a minister I think you sit in cabinet and you discuss with your colleagues...and you have direct participation from both your colleagues and the president. When you are an ambassador you are out there on your own and you've got to be literally on your toes and your wits about you because there's nobody to be asking, 'by the way, what can I say here?'* She also provided examples of the challenges of working in other patriarchal societies, but coming from a government that is comparatively more gender-sensitive, *Italy is one of the most patriarchal. So the men that come to work at the embassy come from this society and the women that come to work come from this society, and you've got to teach them literally that it's not like that here, this is South Africa [in the embassy]. Like for instance we have once a month the Happy Friday, and it tended to be women that cook and things and the men don't (Interview with the author, Pretoria, 2014).* In this instance, she brought South Africa's policy of gender equality with her to her posting, taking it upon herself to implement gender equality amongst the embassy employees. This is a form of impact, by an individual critical actor, on a site that is not examined in the popular research on women and political leadership in South Africa.

Examples such as this are difficult to measure and aggregate. For example, with national legislatures studies have explored the relationship between descriptive and substantive representation to determine the relationship there. The challenge going forward is how do we come up with new ways of exploring women's impact in different spaces and different positions? How do we examine the quality of representation in the diverse political spaces that women occupy?

Do we only look at their impact in terms of women's and gender issues, or do we look at their general impact on their societies?

Challenges

Not only is there the challenge of finding new ways of exploring impact, the fundamental over-riding challenge is to change society. Changing people's behaviours and values is very difficult (Britton 2002a). Women MPs have to fight for every little gain they make; the world of politics is still not open to women. They experience constraints at the party level and experience an adversarial media, amongst other challenges (Waring et al. 2000).

In terms of party support, many women politicians expressed being treated equally to men in terms of party support as candidates; there are no special provisions to support women candidates, and that their gender as women was not important in their selection as candidates (Waring et al. 2000). Despite women's constitutional, electoral and representative gains, there is still some male resistance to their leadership. Women interviewed by Britton (2002a) from all parties felt that men support women in politics mostly with rhetoric, but not so much with support or approval. For example, in South Africa's ANC, one interviewee described alarming incidents in which women were encouraged to withdraw their candidacy on the basis of their gender; *like now the women are having problems even within the African National Congress on the quota system. The men phone them, threaten them at night, 'don't allow your name to go [on the list]'. And suddenly one year we were getting a lot of resignations. I asked my colleagues, 'why?' And then I'm angry with the women... I'm not aware [of what is happening] and then I started to follow that the women in fact are under threat that, 'why have you taken these positions; don't you know that I need to have the position so I can get salaries for my children. If you are going to be in this position you and your husband will be earning money' (Interview with the author, Pretoria, 2014).* In other words, men wanted women removed from the candidate lists to create more room for themselves, using the justification (and assumption) that these women have husbands who can provide. Such incidents are alarming because if men will resort to covert, invisible strategies to decrease women's representation for their personal benefit, it begs the question of what else is happening behind the scenes to the women, and the work that they do?

...It must be taken into context because overall the parliamentarians that are

coming in now, men and women, because of the changes and the new environment and the entrenchment of democracy, it's no more about mainly as we came in there as revolutionary. Now they are becoming politicians and there's a difference, and there's a very big gap between a revolutionary and a politician. So overall it's not only the women; it's the environment now that says 20 years on we are politicians. The question of the revolution, we have achieved so much in this revolutionary past, so we can't be stuck on that. But the other thing has happened, a very unfortunate thing that has happened in the women's movement is the death of the women's movement. And people that are getting into politics now...are not your original revolutionaries, these are people that are interested in politics as a career (Interview with the author, Pretoria, 2014).

Confounding the problem is that not all ANC women are interested in women's interests, and not all ANC women represent the same women's constituency. In addition, some use gender to open doors for themselves but are not interested in furthering gender equality (Geisler 2000). *Of course my question is when I meet some of these parliamentarians they don't know anything about gender (Interview with the author, Kigali, 2013).*

While Rwanda's women MPs have a track record of introducing important legislation, the norm is that the executive branch initiates bills, which then move to cabinet, and finally to parliament to be debated and voted on. In 2006 Rwanda's parliament took up less than 1% of the government budget, meaning limited resources available to them in conjunction with the more powerful executive branch (Powley 2006). This is another reason why more attention has to be paid to women in the executive and cabinet to see how much influence they have there.

That being said, Rwanda's parliament has not uncritically obeyed the executive and cabinet. For example, at one point they formed an Ad Hoc Committee to investigate the conditions of street children after being dissatisfied with the way that the Ministry of Local Government (which was headed by a woman) was handling the issue. It has been found that women MPs are often the most vocal and critical of Ministers and the government. Women MPs have also influenced the national budget to increase spending on health infrastructure and education (Powley 2006).

Unfortunately, there is a gap between legislation and implementation. Despite the strong legislation on land rights women still face structural problems such as having no resources to fight for their rights in the courts, not knowing their rights, and many women are in partnerships but unmarried, thereby having no claim on the property of their husband (neither do their illegitimate children) ((Powley 2006). However, as Powley argues, the problems of implementation are not the responsibility of the women alone, but the entire government and society (Powley 2006). Unfortunately, much of the pressure seems to be placed on the women and the government, *Parliament has made progress, cabinet has made progress, there are many women in very key in positions of cabinet...I think generally the public sector has done very well. The public sector and if I can count the legislature, the parliament is part of that. I think where we need more progress and by progress I don't mean 64% but at least something, in the constitution it says 30% at least. I think we need to increase that in the private sector as well. I think that when a policy is implemented normally the public sector implements it faster because they thought about the policy. I think that's really the reason. But I must say that even though that's the case, that the private sector has to catch up, the private sector also has tried. I think if government hadn't led the way it wouldn't be even what we have, it wouldn't be as much as it is, it would be worse. So I think it will come, it will catch up like it is already beginning to show (Interview with the author, Kigali, 2013). .*

Not only in the public sector, but also in the diplomatic core there are challenges, as I alluded to earlier. While coming from gender-sensitive countries ambassadors to other countries still have to battle far-reaching social, structural and cultural norms which make it more difficult for them to perform their work; *And the other thing is that as a woman there's always in the diplomatic core, it's just there, there's a camaraderie amongst the men, they go to have their drinks and that's where we discuss some of the politics. And most of the time in these countries it's men who are ministers, deputy ministers, director generals, and they interact easier with the male ambassadors. And if you are a woman it's going to be very difficult for me to go and invite the deputy minister for drinks. [It's] taken the wrong way. So you've got to be careful that you don't give an impression of other intentions. But at the same time you've got to make these overtures and it's very, very difficult as a woman (Interview with the author, Pretoria, 2014).*

A Rwandan ambassador, though not talking about the issue of gender inequality in her work, did talk about the challenges of representing Rwanda in the international community; *You see when you are in a position of leadership all eyes are on you. There's a high expectation and support...is not commiserate with the pressures that you get. Because when you are in a position of leadership a lot is expected of you in terms of delivery, in terms of conduct...I didn't have any personal challenges...But the challenge is first of all let me say in the case of Rwanda, like when I was an ambassador two years after the genocide, maybe in fact a year and a half; so first of all the issues we had to deal with, very complex issues; that this is the time of the Congo crises, there was a crises in Burundi, the government did not have enough resources. Yet, you're there, you're supposed to perform even better than people/embassies which have been established for the last 50 years with all the resources, with all the trained staff, so on and so forth. I had one councillor, I didn't have a secretary. My embassy was, in terms of diplomatic staff, 3 people. Me and two men. But, the challenge, the issues I had to deal with! At the time, were like ten/fifteen times what the ambassador of the United States had to deal with.* She went on to explain that not only are there numerous issues to deal with, and not enough resources and manpower, but at that particular time there was also the problem of having people recognise the genocide as a genocide, *I think in terms of women in leadership in Rwanda, I think the biggest challenge we had, one, was to get the situation in Rwanda understood. Because people didn't understand at all. It took a very long time for even people to recognise what happened in Rwanda as genocide. Then the local geopolitics and nobody wants you...but it was very complex and we had to deliver with very little resources....I think it is, it is getting much better, but this was a very very challenging situation that we were in at that time. We had a lot of challenges and very limited means, I think the only resource we had was just our determination (Interview with the author, Kigali, 2013).* In other words, the mandates and responsibilities of political and governmental office-holders are contextual, and we have to examine their success/failures within that context, rather than making simplified examinations that consider the relationship between numbers and impact.

In the conflict resolution and mediation sector a South African woman described the extreme reactions of men to having women's involvement, *Sometimes they will walk out of a room, sometimes they won't listen to you because you are a woman. Sometimes they will sit in a meeting like they did to me in Sudan; not a single, only one man spoke, the chairman, he was embarrassed. I think they were not warned about it being a woman. I came with my CEO, I think that put them off – they never came back (Interview with the author, Pretoria, 2014).*

These anecdotes illustrate that the challenges that women politicians face are numerous, diverse, and often contextual, making it hard to make generalised statements. However, it illustrates that all positions come with their own difficulties, and if we are to broaden our understanding of impact, we should also broaden our understanding of what difficulties and obstacles they face, *I think the biggest challenges that a lot of people don't quite understand – they don't understand the essence of leadership. And, in politics there are always politics. You see what I mean? And sometimes if you are too honest, I used to have a Senegalese friend, I used to tell, 'Oh I don't like politics'. He said 'My sister, if you do not play politics, politics will play you'. You see that kind of cynical attitude to leadership? I don't know how I can explain it, but I think the challenge is to play politics positively (Interview with author, Kigali, 2013).*

Conclusion

The topic of women in politics in Rwanda and South Africa is a complex one. While there have been huge strides in institutional reforms and legislation, implementation and accountability have become some of the most pressing issues. What mechanisms can be put in place to ensure that someone (not necessarily women politicians) becomes accountable for ensuring that rhetoric and policy translate into real changes on the ground? Perhaps projects like Imhigo can be models for creating innovative, contextually driven accountability solutions. Yet, considering that there are already so many institutions that have been created (such as NMGs), there would be no purpose in creating new systems and institutions if those that already exist are already underfunded and over-stretched.

In addition, to understand women's roles and impact in politics and on the society, we should move from the descriptive vs. substantive debate, and develop new ways of exploring women in politics by looking at the diverse kinds of impact that they might make. For example, there should be an examination of the influence that women have within the parties, as well as the influence of women in the executive, and other important positions outside of the parliaments. Once we shift the debate to positions outside of the parliament, we would be able to identify other spaces and ways in which women politicians are challenged in their work, how they overcome them (for example, Rwanda's use of culture), and what differences they make in their various roles (if at all). The anecdotes provided in the last section of this chapter illustrate not only the numerous challenges that women politicians face, but also the impacts that they have, that are perhaps not as recognised because they are not overtly related to women's interests, but are still important for the society as a whole.

Chapter 4: Early Life Experiences and Post-Conflict Transformation Priorities

'When we're talking of equality we're saying the society is structurally not okay. It's not discrimination we're fighting against; we're fighting against lack of equality.'

Exploring or classifying a state (e.g. capitalist or patriarchal state), is done by examining how a particular group or class of people have been affected by that government (Molyneux 1985). In this chapter I suggest that the type of state and its priorities are influenced by the experiences of those participating in the state apparatus. I especially examine the early life experiences of the women that I interviewed to determine what role that has played in their political priorities today.

A perspective regarding women's interests is that women have different perceptions, which are determined by their upbringing or biology, or both. As a result, they behave differently to men and have different leadership styles. In her study, Mtintso's women and men participants do indeed believe that women bring different agendas to parliament, such as a greater emphasis on socio-economic and human rights. On the other hand, there are those who believe that there can be no sisterhood of women; women experience different forms of gendered oppression because they have other social identities, such as class and race (Mtintso 2003).

In this chapter, I argue that it is the early life experiences before reaching formal political positions that inform the priorities of the leadership of the respective governments. *I think definitely your life experience influences you...if you've met challenges...in your life you'll recognise those challenges in others, and you understand them better. Like I said, in leadership really the important thing is to serve and to work with the people. But if you see poor people or disadvantaged people, if you have had that experience you are most likely to understand it better than somebody who has never had that experience. And in that case you are less likely to blame them than somebody who just...see people who are in a bad situation and you blame them, 'why are they poor, it's because they are lazy, it's because this or that, why can't they do this?' But if you have experienced it then you know the constraints that stop them from being able to do that and then if you're working on programs you're likely to be able to address these constraints. This is from the negative side (Interview with the author, Kigali, 2013).* In other words, one is better able to relate to others if they have shared experiences. Life experiences thus become lessons which would later influence one's decisions. *But also from a positive side...I travelled a lot; I have worked in different countries both in Africa and in Europe, so you learn a lot from your experience. And now if you're going to be taking decisions, making programs, you're not going to start from down there. You have seen what works, you have seen what doesn't work. So you're life experience, really, is very important, it's part of who you are, it shapes your character (Interview with the author, Kigali, 2013).* According to this participant, life experiences not only affect choices later in life, but also who you are in terms of what you believe.

A South African woman explained the influence of conflict on the perspectives of women politicians. *One of the interesting things which I think is an experience for not just me, you'll find across the board for women parliamentarians and executives, is that particularly South Africa being a society post conflict, we are very conscious about issues of exclusion and marginalisation and issues of women's empowerment – so all those came into there (Interview with the author, Pretoria, 2014).* This is an example of an experience that is relevant to both the Rwandan and South African contexts as both have experienced conflict. She is explaining that the factors that led to conflict, particularly in South Africa, become important political priorities. Indeed, in the IPU survey it was found that most women who enter politics do so with the motivation of wanting to bring change to their communities and societies, with a particular emphasis on social justice (Waring et al., 2000). *When we're talking of equality we're saying the society is structurally not okay. It's not discrimination we're fighting against; we're fighting against lack of equality. Apartheid was not about discrimination, it wasn't about racial discrimination (Interview with the author, Johannesburg, 2014).*

Women's Interests vs. Gender Neutrality

One commonality that has emerged through my interviews is that women politicians see their roles holistically. They have not self-imposed restrictions in terms of which constituencies or groups to represent. *Like when we are dealing with women's issues, as I can say, yeah it's good because if you are a woman you understand your fellow woman, but it's not always about that. Women should be there to perform all their tasks, but not only for women, but also for the government (Interview with the author, Kigali, 2013).* Women representatives around the world feel that they have a responsibility to represent the interests of the entire electorate; to represent only women means to exclude the interests of men or other groups. They feel that they are elected by all voters, and so must represent the interests of everyone (Waring et al. 2000). *Now, whether that number means that there will be more favourable decisions for women; I don't think it's necessarily true because at the end of the day these days there's very few gender specific legislations that we bring, we want to give equal opportunity to men and women, so as much as possible the laws should all be equal for men and women or it should be able to make sense to man and woman. Even if it affects women more or men it should be able to make sense to man and woman (Interview with the author, Kigali, 2013).* In essence, women politicians are concerned with creating free societies in which the genders are equal, and not one favoured over the other. *But I want to also emphasise that as feminists our change is definitely, as African feminists, our change is really about the society: women must make choices that girls and boys, women and men can fulfil their potential and make choices about their lives. So it's not just a women only, it's not that type of radical feminism (Interview with the author, Kigali, 2013).* The choice to specifically represent women's interests comes from an awareness of gender inequality. While women politicians try to practice gender neutrality, they also feel that they are in a position to better understand the needs of women, which men cannot do (Waring et al. 2000).

Ultimately, these women are not interested in making some changes here-and-there. They view their mandate as being much larger and far-reaching than that. *But this thing is the whole organisation of society. So what we're talking about is the reorganisation, the rethinking about society (Interview with the author, Johannesburg, 2014).*

Their own experiences indicate that this is not a simple process, nor an easy one, and that it requires a great deal of consciousness and thoughtfulness. *One time we tested with SAFM. They wanted to change the programme calling all farmers, so I said I will use that as a test case…we asked farmers, both men and women. It was very interesting that the house was split into two: men had no problem whatever time it was moved to. Women had a serious concern, so I asked women, 'why are you having a problem?' They said, '…even now, we are not the beneficiaries of that message because it comes at five o'clock. Me at 5am I'm up, I'm preparing food for this man, I'm preparing the kids for school, so I don't have time to listen to any message that might be in calling all farmers at the time. When the kids go I must clean after them before I take my hoe to go and plant in the garden. In the afternoon when I come back it's the same story.' So if you ask me what is the best time, all of them without exception, they said just before seven o'clock in the evening or after seven. I said, why? They said because around that time I'm either eating sitting down, I can have a moment of hearing your messages (Interview with the author, Pretoria, 2014).*

Below I will attempt to illustrate that the Rwanda refugee experience, and the South African experience of Apartheid, were definitive educational experiences for the women that I interviewed. These experiences ultimately shaped their politics.

Rwanda has been accused of being an authoritarian regime under the RPF led government, of practicing human rights' abuses, of silencing dissent and opposing views, of exploiting the guilt of the international community for the lack of action during the genocide, and of controlling civil society and the judiciary (Reyntjens 2006, Reyntjens 2011). Freedom House has ranked Rwanda as 'Not Free', because of a repression of opposition parties, civil society members, and journalists, as well as a flawed presidential election in 2010. That being said, the government has been praised for its commitment to gender equality, though there are voices that argue that this commitment is not significant due to the authoritarian nature of the government (Debusscher & Ansoms 2013). In 1995 it was reported that there were extrajudicial executions, disappearances, and massacres of civilians by the RPF. It is also reported that during the 1990s and 2000s a wave of Hutu politicians fled the country, as well as Tutsi genocide survivors (Burnet 2008). According to Burnet, the RPF has defended itself against accusations of authoritarian rule by arguing the interests of good governance and security (Burnet 2008).

To understand contemporary politics in Rwanda today, it is important to understand the exile and refugee experience before 1994, and the international responses to the political and humanitarian crises thereof (Long 2012). Most of Rwanda's post-1994 'returnees' are well-educated Tutsis who grew up outside of Rwanda. Most are in Kigali and work in the business and administrative sectors (McLean Hilker 2011). Many of those who have returned to Rwanda after being refugees before the war have taken up important positions in government, civil society and international organisations (Herndon & Randell 2013). According to Debusscher & Ansoms (2013) their work is influenced by the concepts and ideas that they gained from the rest of the world. All but one of the Rwandan women that I interviewed grew up outside of Rwanda as refugees, returning in their adulthood. As a result, I spend more time examining this history then I do the nuances of the genocide (though the two histories cannot be separated).

Structurally, Rwanda's government consists of the ruling RPF with a coalition of smaller political parties. The parties that are not a part of the coalition also cooperate with the government, rather than form a strong opposition (Devlin & Elgie 2008). There is a criticism against Kagame, that he is enabling women's leadership not out of a commitment to gender equality, but because he wants the loyalty of this majority constituency. There is also the criticism that he uses women in these positions as tools for his own agenda (Powley 2006). The main criticism of Rwanda's gender policies are that they are done to attract donor funding because gender issues are in fashion, and Rwanda's national budget is heavily dependent on donor funding (Debusscher & Ansoms 2013). When asked about this, one woman not only defended her country, but also defended herself (and other women) as not being window-dressing, but of being influential and participatory actors. *Who are we pleasing? That we are window dressing? Why don't they do it? I don't think so, because if that was the case I think that everybody would do it. And I don't think we are even getting any more money than anybody because we have women in our parliament. So we are not doing anything for anybody, to tell you the truth...Whatever we do we do it for ourselves. But I know that there are some things we do and we are opposed, even building a hotel like this, including women in the life of this country, in the public life of this country. But I don't think we are doing it for anybody. I don't think I was given a job as a woman to window dress. I'm not here for window dressing. But you know I am not one of the top most women and we have but we have the speakers, we've had women speakers of parliament successively. I don't think we are window dressing otherwise what would we want our parliament to do if it is headed by a woman, it's like we don't want our parliament to work. Then for the 64% of women in parliament, those are parliamentarians that we spend a lot of money on them in the national budget. Why should we spend money to window dress? You know, I don't think we are being, I don't think people who are saying that are being fair. Actually they are being unfair (Interview with the author, Kigali, 2013).* The essence of this argument is that if Rwanda was doing things for appearance purposes then the country wouldn't be able to function. People (in this case, women) would be unsuitable for the positions they are in.

The Rwandan women expressed the belief that the accusation that they are part of a donor-funding manipulation by the government stems from people's internalised belief that it is impossible to have many effective women in political leadership. *But on the other hand, I think countries have failed to recognise the importance and the potential of women. So in covering up their own failures they have to get, they have to get an explanation why we are doing so. Actually I wish I could ask why they do not have this 50/50 percent women? Why don't they? Now for them they are not even progressing, and they believe in human rights. Well, they say they believe in human rights (Interview with the author, Kigali, 2013).*

Another woman explained that doubts concerning women's representation are an issue that all women in politics face, not only in Rwanda. *This is the struggle of all women in the world. So they are viewed as not capable. They are viewed as s caretaker of the family, take care of the kids, cook. The western countries, as time goes by, they will also realise it is not just about the number, it's about performance. Yeah, it is not only the western countries; it's even Africa, even Rwanda. People saying they are not capable but when they are there they realise they are capable (Interview with the author, Kigali, 2013).* This response is slightly more optimistic because it displays a belief that attitudes regarding women's political leadership might change once women have proven themselves outside of the home. The previous two responses, on the other hand, indicate the belief that accusations against Rwanda's leadership are more political in nature, than attitudinal. Not only is there a scepticism regarding the political intentions of increasing women's representation, but there is indeed doubt about the quality of the representation.

Debusscher & Ansoms (2013) argue that there are fundamental flaws in Rwanda's commitment to gender equality, which is that there is only a commitment if the objectives further the economic development priority of the country. They argue that there is an over-emphasis of an economic rationale; those working in subsistence farming and care work are overlooked, there is a focus on quantitative gender indicators – not quality, and that civil society does not have the freedom to influence policy, and finally, that there is a lack of grassroots participation.

While their points are valid and important, I take a different position, which will become evident in this and the following chapter. President Kagame understands that using women in the development programme of the country is important because they constitute more than half of the country's population, constituting important labour capital for the country (Uwineza & Pearson 2009; Debusscher & Ansoms 2013). *And our President has said it so many times…this is what he says and this is what I believe; 1; it is their right, it's their right. 2; women are more than 50% of this country, if we really want to develop we cannot leave half of the population aside, and I know the leadership of this country is for development. It is for people's well-being and you cannot do it if you leave the other half away, at least this is what we believe (Interview with the author, Kigali, 2013).*

She provided a simple example of how Rwanda has been criticised in the past, only to find that their judgement was correct. *You know when we were building this hotel (Serena)…it was in 2004, the international community was making noise, 'no Rwanda is too poor to have a hotel like this'. I mean the comments they make, of course when it's finished now you see how full it is, you know. So I'm only giving that as an example (Interview with the author, Kigali, 2013).* This was a hotel in which I was staying during my visit to the country, and it was extremely busy while I was there. Not only was it hosting tourists, but also conferences and other events. A logical analysis would be that this hotel has created employment, amongst other economic contributions.

For an impoverished country such as Rwanda, why shouldn't economic growth be a national priority, especially given the way economic downturns and high unemployment was a contributing factor to the genocide (van der Meeren 1996; Schindler 2009)? Secondly, it is surely a positive thing that women's contributions are being recognised and harnessed. If the country's economy improves, while this would not be an automatic solution for gender equality, it would surely improve many women's quality of life in a society where women are gaining more rights to become independent. *So when you see Rwanda is developing it is because it is using the strength of the women and the man. Not only the men to work for the rest of the people...We are pushing, our economic growth is going so high within the region, it is because everybody is working (Interview with the author, Kigali, 2013).*

The second criticism that Debusscher & Ansoms (2013) make is that those performing care work and subsistence agriculture are overlooked. In my view, this is the experience of women around the world, and is not unique to Rwanda. However, the fact that the government is not getting it right on every single issue is not an indication that they are not committed to gender equality.

The third criticism of Debusscher & Ansoms (2013) is that the government depends more on quantitative indicators, rather than the quality of change. In this regard, in my view, Rwanda is ahead of other countries by setting clearly defined objectives, and designating the responsible ministries and departments for meeting those objectives (as discussed in previous chapters), which is important for transparency and accountability. Not to say that quality is not important, but that quantitative indicators are important too. Indeed, according to one woman interviewed, Rwanda emphasises implementation and accountability. *The laws manage everything. And in Rwanda a law is a law, it must be implemented. It's not like other countries where things are on papers, it is their constitution, they talk very good things, but when it comes to implementation it is a different issue, but in Rwanda the law is the law. It has to be implemented...if you go to these income generating activities, when you go to market, many women are working there, which formerly everything was being done by men. Is that wanting a donation? Isn't it doing something by having a big number of women? A local woman now knows how to go to the bank, which they didn't know. Formerly a woman was not even supposed to supposed to open a bank account without consulting the husband (Interview with the author, Kigali, 2013).*

While criticisms have been made against Kagame (as indicated above) the women I interviewed spoke highly of him. While discussing her family's feelings about her appointment to an executive position in government, one woman said. *Well, very excited because our government, led by our President Paul Kagame, is very progressive. It's a government that liberated Rwanda and it is a government that over the last 20 years has really shown that it's committed to improving the people's lives, so people trust the government. And so working for government is a privilege. And because it's a government that works, that is really why it's a privilege. So when the appointment happened and when my government, my family saw that the president of the country and the government had entrusted me it was an honour and privilege and they saw it that way and that's why they were very excited (Interview with the author, Kigali, 2013).* This is another response which emphasises the effectiveness of the government.

Another interviewee described Kagame as a visionary leader. *But I attribute it to his Excellency, he is a visionary leader, I am telling you. Even for us, we say, but how does he think of these things? Is it God is talking to him directly, there are times where we also wonder… (Interview with the author, Kigali, 2013).* Indeed, a contextual understanding of leadership may be required to understand Rwandan politics. For example, according to Herndon & Randell (2013), what to the outside may appear to be an authoritarian regime, on the inside may be viewed as a strong, decisive and effective leadership.

One interviewee pointed to the central issue, that women's access and participation in formal politics depends on the government and senior leadership. Without a commitment from them, it is hard to make gains for women. *I am saying all this depends on leadership…But the ones from the top,[if] they say no who else will say it when the top man says no? So it is the political will of the government… (Interview with the author, Kigali, 2013).* In particular, it is the leadership of Kagame that has enabled women's leadership. It is interesting that this response places particular emphasis on the idea that if the senior leadership is against women's leadership, then it is harder for those outside of leadership structures to make it possible. Perhaps what is concerning is the over-identification with the approval of senior leadership, rather than civil society or grassroots movement. This might be an example of Herndon & Randell (2013) argument that we have to understand Rwanda's politics contextually, rather than super-impose outside perceptions of what politics and governance should look and be like. In fact, this follows the previous responses I cited earlier in response to accusations of women's leadership as window-dressing. The responses essentially argue that the criticisms are attitudinal regarding women's leadership, rather than legitimate concerns.

Another criticism of contemporary Rwanda, made by McLean Hilker (2011) is that the Rwandan government has created a new official history of Rwanda. This history is said to be created through the use of gacaca courts, the media, genocide memorials and re-education camps for ex-soldiers and students called ingando. This assertion is problematic because it assumes that a particular narrative is being asserted through the justice system, the memorials, etc. as if Rwanda is not to have these. In the same way that Germany's laws do not permit Holocaust denial, so Rwanda does not permit genocide denial (Herndon & Randell 2013). In an effort to foster unity and combat divisions Rwanda is trying to eliminate the ethnic identities of Hutu, Tutsi and Twa. Since 2001 it has created several laws in an attempt to do so; a law to punish those who participate in genocide, crimes against humanity, war crimes, a law on discrimination and sectarianism, and a law that criminalises genocide ideology. Unfortunately, there are still challenges in this regard. For example, an enquiry in 2007 found that there are schools that still teach the pre-genocide curriculum and make students wear different uniforms based on ethnicity – examples which legitimise the need for a concerted effort eliminate ethnic divisions. That being said, critics of Rwanda have argued that these laws have been abused to enable the government to silence human rights organisations, ban opposing political parties and prevent criticism (McLean Hilker 2011). As discussed in previous chapters, the ethnic identifications of Hutu, Tutsi and Twa were fluid during pre-colonial times, and have become contentious since they were cemented by colonial administrations. In later years Rwanda might then be an example of the outcome of attempting to eliminate colonial era attitudes and classifications that persisted after independence. Indeed, we have to question criticisms that state that a country is not allowed to alter its official history to be more inclusive and reconciliatory. As discussed previously, the colonial powers tried to reconstruct Rwandan history along ethnic lines. For this reason, a new history is a requirement. Unfortunately, whether this new history is accurate or not is outside of the scope of this book.

South Africa is also doubted and criticised internationally, as a South African ambassador explained to me. *Most difficult for me is selling South Africa to people that are negative and especially business, because...they want quick returns and we are a new democracy. They still have doubts about us as a black government. There's doubt about our leadership and all kinds of things – so you've got to sell South Africa – and there are many, many people that are selling their countries out there...competing there selling your country so that business can go to your country, and that I found very, very challenging (Interview with the author, Pretoria, 2014).* Indeed, South Africa's political leadership is not only doubted by the international community, but internally as well. In South Africa there is the argument, by feminists, that women politicians are more loyal to their parties than to women or feminism. However, just because the country is democratic, does not mean that racial inequalities no longer exist. The political parties of the ANC and SACP are the best institutions that embody commitments to gender, race and class equality. Furthermore, the women representatives' political legitimacy arises from their election, and not from their gender. Their mandate is determined by the policies that their parties campaigned on (Mtintso 2003). Mtintso (2003) conducted a study which found that women MPs are concerned with addressing the needs for which they were elected, but their daily experiences as women is the point from which they try to understand gender inequality. She believes that if society is to be transformed, then theory and practice must combine to address the real (not just theoretical) challenges that women face; there needs to be an understanding of the connections of different kinds of oppressions and inequalities, which is something that is sometimes missed amongst those who feel that South Africa's women politicians are not representing ordinary women (Mtintso 2003).

An ANC member I interviewed has questioned the party's current commitment to gender equality. However, she did not take the stance of accusing those women leaders of merely being window-dressing. *But I also must tell you that I am so disenchanted with what I see, that, yes, I was with the first group, I was there until 1999, the first group of parliamentarians. Pregs also resigned; Lynne Brown is resigning now in April. The question is: how do you have an effective strategic role as a woman in your political party where the political party has got so much power, but they are also so geared to a particular political agenda that women's issues are actually either just used to promote the party agenda or they're not serious about it. And that is my problem – like if we have an ANC Women's League, is that a voting fodder or is that a strategic structure?(Interview with the author, Kigali, 2013).* In other words, even if the ANC's commitment to gender equality is decreasing, and women are being used to amass votes, the women are participating (just not in the way that feminists would want them to). The problem is that, according to this interviewee, the ANC Women's League is not participating in decision-making, nor is it advancing an agenda that speaks to women's needs.

While Rwanda's government is accused of being too involved in constructing an 'official' history and emphasising its violent past, on the other hand, in the South African context, Graybill (2001) argues that there has been no formal, systemised discussion of the structural violence and lingering repercussions of Apartheid (such as women's disproportionate experience of poverty) in the way that individual human rights abuses were addressed at the TRC. This despite the ways in which Apartheid's legacy continues, particularly for Black women. *Everything; our geography, where we live today, where we shop today, all of this is still defined by the geography of apartheid (Interview with author, Johannesburg, 2014).* In addition, Black women are still largely marginalised in South Africa's society, whereas white women are more advantaged (Mtintso, 2003). A prominent leader in South Africa, Thenjiwe Mtintso, has conducted a study where she interviewed female and male MPs as well as civil society gender activists. She makes the argument that there are no universal women's interests that can be represented by a particular group in parliament, for reasons such as the varying social positions of women determined by their racial and class identities. Black women experienced a triple oppression of race, class, and gender. Influx control kept most Black women in the homelands where there was little employment. There was overcrowding on the land, affecting agricultural productivity. Many women were dependent on money sent by husbands from the urban areas, and sometimes men found new wives and had new families, and stopped taking care of those left in the rural areas (Graybill, 2001). In other words, the experiences of different women in South Africa vary tremendously, and addressing issues of race and class, for example, would simultaneously address the interests of Black women, the most oppressed demographic in South Africa.

Indeed, some women politicians from around the world feel the need to represent the interests of women because of their belief that women are discriminated against. Some are also conscious of the intersections of other social injustices such as class and race (Waring et al 2000). Similarly, women MPs interviewed by Mtintso (2003) expressed that the ANC is the party that is committed to representing the interests of the poorest in society. The majority of the poor are women in the townships and rural areas. Some women who are in parliament today come from that background, or have an understanding of the conditions and have a commitment to change them (Mtintso 2003). *The women in the rural areas those days were without their husbands because many of their husbands were working in the mines, especially that part the Eastern Cape where I came from. And these women would come to my home in the afternoons to assist with the weeding – you plough the mielies, you plough the beans, you plough the pumpkins, and then you have the weeding season. And the women will come with their hoes...But then when they come in the afternoon, these women, they come not for money but they would be paid by getting sugar and tea. So they will do the hoeing, the removing of the weeds for two hours and then after that they are all going to get (Interview with the author, Pretoria, 2014).* This anecdote illustrates the sheer poverty that women in the rural areas experienced under Apartheid.

Not only where the living conditions of the women difficult, but their lack of education, and the Apartheid state's laws and regulations made life extraordinarily difficult for them. For example, the Influx control laws regulated who could reside in the urban areas and who was to stay in the rural areas. In the process families were split up when men were allowed in the urban areas but their wives and children were not (Graybill 2001). *And then later on when I could write letters, that was one of my responsibilities', that they would come to my mother and they would ask if I could write letters on their behalf, those who could not write, to their husbands. And I remember my mother telling me that when I write these letters I must never tell anybody what the contents of the letters [are]. I wasn't sure exactly why but I didn't because it was one of those things (Interview with the author, Pretoria, 2014).*

She went on to explain the other obstacles they faced within this system, and how women were not only subject to the laws, but also to the whims of the administrators. *Then there was apartheid and it was harder. Women in South Africa, we would go to offices, accompany them because they needed permits to visit their husbands in urban areas. In some cases for no reason this permit is refused. And then the women, their husbands would die and then there would be a crisis...I worked particularly in KwaZulu-Natal where the law of inheritance was such they were deprived of anything; they wouldn't inherit anything from their husbands. In fact, in the urban area if you had acquired furniture, the in-laws had the rights within the law....[it] was called the Natal Code of Law. It had to do with the inheritance laws in Natal. Women were minors and women could not even sign a contract.* In other words, Black women were doubly oppressed in terms of race and class. Such injustices were not only experienced by illiterate rural women, but also professional Black women – illustrating that economic status could not enable one to transcend one's racial or gender category under the Apartheid system. *Because I lived in Natal as a professional woman, I was a minor. When I wanted to buy furniture as a member of the furniture shop because I lived, I had a room I had acquired – the furniture shop couldn't give me the furniture; there was a big problem because I was a minor....So you have that, and then on the other hand you go to a shop those days and they are not allowing you in some of the shops to try a dress on because you are black' (Interview with the author, Pretoria, 2014).* In other words, women experienced a triple-oppression. They experienced economic poverty, gender inequality, and racial inequality on a daily basis. Even women who were economically advantaged could not completely benefit from it because their race and gender provided obstacles.

As one interviewee explained, it was not possible to be a Black South African and not be affected by the inequalities and injustices that were taking place. *Everybody. But this is what I say in my generation certainly you couldn't miss what was going on in the country, so it was automatic. You see, in the 1930s, 1940s, 1950s, you couldn't be a Black South African and not react to Apartheid – it was as simple as that. Now in the family we used to talk; at that time you had in an organised way you had the South African Indian Congress or a Transvaal Indian Congress, a Natal Indian Congress, which was formed before the ANC, it was formed by Mahatma Ghandi. Indians for example could not go to the Free State (Interview with the author, Johannesburg, 2014).* As this and the previous examples illustrate, Apartheid pervaded every aspect of life that it was impossible to be unaffected by its inequalities and injustices.

These were felt from early childhood. *I was brought up in Cape Town; I was born in Cape Town. I lived in an area called Maitland. I think what was probably the first consciousness was the way the Group Areas affected people – that was really the most stark awareness of movement of people and friends and family suddenly, you know the break up, uprooting of people. I have a very stark memory of probably being like three or four years old and I didn't really know Cape Town at all but we had an incredibly beautiful drive around the peninsula, and as you come from Hout Bay and you can see Noordhoek beach down below – and I said to my parents, 'That's my favourite beach and we're going there.' 'We can't.' And I just couldn't understand it, I said, 'What do you mean?' 'No, we can't go.' And I'd say, 'But why do you say that?' 'Oh, no, we're not the right -.' You know, they were trying to explain very awkwardly and uncomfortable and all sorts of things. I said, 'But what are you doing about it?' And they said, 'No, but it's the law of the land.' I said, 'Well, I'm going to do something about it (Interview with the author, Kigali, 2013).*

One woman had had the benefit of having grown up inside and outside of South Africa, thereby being able to contrast two different societies. *...But also my mom is Swazi, so part of my early years I spent in Swaziland and Swaziland was under the British protectorate, as you know, and Swaziland then got their independence in the 1960s. So I grew up in Swaziland without the notion of race and colour and Swaziland expatriates, white people who were sneaking into Swaziland – so there was not a 'them' and 'us' kind of thing, and there was no preferences of white; we went to the same schools. So I think the reality shocked us when coming to South Africa and you found that you couldn't go to public toilets, certain public toilets, those are for whites. Huh? And I think that started to make you feel something is wrong in the society (Interview with the author, Pretoria, 2014).*

Another South African woman expressed being acutely aware of the limitations she faced as a result of her race. *You would go to a beach and you'd say I want to go on that merry-go-round. You can't go. Why? Because it's only for whites. So there was no way you could not be aware, especially if you were in an urban area but I'm sure it happened in rural areas as well. And it was across white-black, whether it was Indian or coloured or African – there were subdivision and some distinctions – so everybody was aware (Interview with the author, Johannesburg, 2014).*

Perhaps what comes through from these stories is not just the unfairness, from the perspective of a child, but a feeling of deprivation as well; not being able to go on the beach, not being able to use certain toilets, not being able to enjoy swings on a park. These indicate that they not only felt the divisions, but the inequalities in the divisions as well.

Other types of inequalities were also experienced in early childhood, as well as a sense of the injustice and unfairness thereof. In this instance, an awareness of gendered inequalities, and women's lower status in society is experienced as an adolescent girl. *My father had died when I was two years. And when I moved to the Eastern Cape, again it was a female-headed household, my uncle had died. And two significant things happened in my life at that time when I was a child. One was that in the Eastern Cape my uncle died and my aunt was being asked to marry the brother to the uncle...She was asked to do this but she resisted and because she resisted we were kicked out of that village and we went to stay in another village with my aunt. And at that village again we were harassed because there was a claim that she was a witch and that's why she was kicked out from the first village to the second village. That raised questions for me as to – at that time I was about 14 – how you could be made to marry somebody who is your relative and somebody that you have never been in love with? So those questions as a child arose (Interview with the author, Pretoria, 2014).* While this experience was not a consequence of Apartheid, it shows the cultural inequalities that existed, particularly on the basis of gender.

The same woman also became aware of class differences early on, and how they were influenced by race. While there wasn't yet the comprehension and language to articulate it, a sense of things being wrong was acutely felt. *And the second one was when I was in Johannesburg...there was a lady called Mrs Minty and my aunt was working for Mrs Minty and I used to go to my aunt's work on a Thursday in the morning to go and fetch her because she'd be bringing leftovers and things like that. So I would not go to school on Thursday; go to my aunt. And Mrs Minty had a huge house, very huge, and she had I think about four cats and two dogs and no children. And at home we were about 11 and we had only one bedroom. We were a very happy family, to the extent that I didn't know who was my biological brother or sister in this; we were just family. But Mrs Minty, there she was, one room for Mrs Minty to share with us, take some of us, we can stay with her, she's lonely. And my sister explained the question of apartheid: black and white and why Mrs Minty stays alone. And this struck me as completely unfair, not only for us as blacks but for Mrs Minty (Interview with the author, Pretoria, 2014).*

She described developing an awareness of three problems which she faced, being Black, being a woman and being poor. *So all these things were making no sense to me but I was understanding that the problem was being a woman, the problem was being black. There's a problem with being poor because also now that I was staying in Orlando East but there was a place called Dube where people were slightly richer and they were living a better life than we in Orlando. So all these dynamics, at that time they were not yet formulated into theoretical terms of class, race and gender... (Interview with the author, Pretoria, 2014).*

In addition, family members, such as her mother, had a role in developing her consciousness, but also that injustice does not have to be accepted. Here she relates her mother's personal experience, which served as a lesson within her own life. *One day she was working at Baragwaneth Hospital sewing the uniforms of nurses when they are torn...And she had a boss that was Ma Aminis. And Ma Aminis was quite bossy and quite white and apartheid-thinking. And one day, I don't know what she had done to my mother, but she had insulted my mother and she had a private toilet, Ma Aminis. When Ma Aminis was in the toilets because she didn't have to lock it, she just left outside, my mother got in to the toilet, beat Ma Aminis, got out, locked the toilet, took her bag and went back home and kept quiet and told us that you must never allow anybody to walk over you. Never, never, don't allow that; it doesn't matter how poor you were. (Interview with the author, Pretoria, 2014).*

On the other hand, one woman was encouraged in the other direction, by her community. Members of her community encouraged her to not get involved in politics, and to accept the status quo. She was detained in solitary confinement during Apartheid, but was not supported by family members. They viewed her imprisonment as that of a criminal, and not a political activist. *And the fact that some of my family probably looked at disdain the fact that I was in prison. I remember going to church after being freed and one church elder said to me, 'I hope you'll behave yourself in the future' (Interview with the author, Kigali, 2013).*

It was not only the experiences within South Africa that were a contributing factor to political priorities. Life was difficult for those in exile as well. ANC members survived on meagre funding for the ANC, and most did not have salaried jobs (Hassim, 2004). Additionally, the exile experience is sometimes viewed as dangerous and demoralising. However, this is not always the case. Exile can provide protection and external support (Lodge, 1987). For one woman, like many others, exile became a means of survival. *Then of course the Lesotho massacre happened, it happened at the time when I was in Cuba. Anyway, I came back but then soon it was quite clear that I was either going to be a victim or...No, it was not either; the question of being a victim was always there...if Lesotho got to know about me and the work that I do. So they requested the ANC to withdraw me. I was withdrawn from Lesotho and I then went to Botswana; then I worked under comrade A there and then I was promoted to being the commander. And it was mainly because of the experience, discipline (Interview with the author, Pretoria, 2014).* While men and women were in exile together, their experiences therein are different in some ways, because of their genders and the inequalities they experienced within the movement.

The different perceptions of democracy within society, and within the ANC, are influenced by different experiences (Suttner, 2003). The ideologies of earlier ANC members, such as the 1940's Youth League were based on mass populist and militant campaigns. From the same age group there were working class leaders, some of whom were also involved in the South African Communist Party (SACP), who held radical socio-economic ideologies. Then there is a younger generation who were more involved in clandestine operations than mass based campaigns. Finally, there was another group of men who were more experienced in the bureaucracy of the movement and who had attended foreign universities (Lodge 1987). It is important to note that while Lodge (1987) provides an analysis of the different types of men and ideological groups in the ANC in exile, the analysis lacks the ideology of women members, and what groups they constituted.

After 1976 MK saw an increase in women recruits, so that there were 20% women by 1991. Some of these women had been leaders in the movement against Apartheid within South Africa's borders, and were quite militant. Women's involvement in MK is credited with helping to open up discourses about women's positions in the movement, and brought an increased recognition of women's contributions. Women had had to prove themselves, and were able to gain respect through their capabilities (Hassim 2004). Here a former MK commander explains the attitudes of male soldiers towards women's involvement, and how women had to navigate those attitudes. *Fundamentally it's there, 'women don't belong to the army; these circumstances are quite bad but we accept them, poor things, what can we do?' And from there arises again other dimensions. 'Because they don't belong here they can't cope, we know, they really can't cope'. Or, 'because they belong here we should share and assist them. But if they can't cope we should assist them or we should watch – they're going to fail'. So as women we then had to take decisions – one, as much as we were not feminists in our thinking, but we've got to unite and defend ourselves and prove ourselves. So you had this consistently. You've got to prove yourself; prove that in fact you can even be better than the men themselves (Interview with the author, Pretoria, 2014).*

Rwandan women were also members of their armed struggle (Kantengwa 2010). They were able to gain the respect of men through their involvement in the armed wing of the RPF. *There were not a lot of women, but they were there, even women soldiers were there. And civilians too. I think that's how even it came to be that in the government they want to put women in that side. Those who went in the military, they would train, they we were able like men, so they were appointed in military posts, and they served well (Interview with the author, Kigali, 2013).*

The RPF was founded in exile as a liberation movement by the Rwandan diaspora after 40 years of exclusion from Rwanda. The liberation movement was characterised by a need for political and economic rights, social justice and a need for national identity and belonging (Kantengwa 2010). Men who were refugees and/or in exile had experienced discrimination, and so were able to understand the concept of gender equality and to viewed it in the same way that they understood Tutsi discrimination and ethnic inequalities (Powley 2006).

120 000 Rwandan Tutsis were refugees outside of Rwanda between 1959 and 1963 (van der Meeren 1996). *We grew up in, some in refugee camps, some in different circumstances. Life was not easy (Interview with the author, Kigali, 2013).* For those who grew up as refugees outside of Rwanda, their experiences were about their refugee/foreigner status, and the backlash that they experienced from host populations. For example, Uganda, where the RPF was founded, hosted approximately 200 000 Rwandan refugees who began to be victimised by the Obote regime in the late 1960's, and again in the 1980's civil war. In one region of Uganda about 60 000 Rwandan refugees were killed. Rwandans then joined Museveni's National Resistance Army (NRM) to help get rid of their mutual enemy, Obote. In 1986, of 14 000 NRM soldiers, 3000 were Rwandan, and many held prominent positions within this army (van der Meeren 1996). Such circumstances would create feelings of needing a sense of security, home, and citizenship. *The way I came to be interested in politics; I was a refugee outside of the country, so like other refugees I wanted to know more about the history of my country, so I was interested in learning about the past. So I joined politics by joining the army, the RPF (Interview with the author, Kigali, 2013).* This participant spent her childhood in the Congo. In the Congo (Zaire) Rwandan refugees experienced more ethnic discrimination than those in other countries. Refugees were harassed, physically attacked and robbed by the police and locals

alike. For political motives, 18 000 Rwandans were killed in an area of Zaire in 1991 (Long 2012; van der Meeren 1996). *Like I said earlier, I was a refugee in Congo, so that was something that was not easy for me, and being a refugee you learn a lot. You pass through struggles...I wanted to have solidarity within me...You see... it was the experience of refugees in the country, people saying, 'You are Rwandan!' They were discriminating, 'You are Rwandese; you don't even belong here!' So you think that you must find your country (Interview with the author, Kigali, 2013).*

The refugees were not only engaged in military liberation activities, but were involved in social upliftment activities as well, and these pre-date the RPF. *Even before the RPF was started, after graduation I actually didn't work in Uganda. I moved to Kenya. So I was working in Kenya. And I lived in Kenya for 13 years. Then while I was in Kenya there were a lot of refugees, Rwandese refugees in areas around the city of Nairobi. So I remember as far back as the early 1980's we started like an association of women, Rwandan women, in Nairobi. And this association, ...the main focus for it was to empower...women refugees, Rwandese women refugees, to try and support them in developing skills so they could do like crafts. You find a market for them. We used to take young girls, they teach them how to dance traditional dance and then we would organise concerts and raise money now to take back into projects for these women. So that was like a social activity, but it was also the beginning of the political activity. Because we were dealing with...Rwandese women to try and improve their situation. And to try and get our children trained in our traditions and so as to retain traditional values and so on and so forth. So you can see there is an element of, its social political activism. So that's actually how we all started, so we all knew each other and then when RPF movement started then we just moved straight on, you know like carried on from what we were doing (Interview with the author, Kigali, 2013).*

In Rwanda today, the dominant ideologies are of unity and reconciliation, including gender unity (Herndon & Randell 2013). Since 1994 they have continued with different activities to reconcile the Rwandan people. *...We still have that reconciliation commission...we have another commission fighting genocide ideology, it is there.... You can't stop it now, it would be too early (Interview with the author, Kigali, 2013).* She went on to explain the reasons for the continued work for reconciliation and unity, as well as the challenges. *Because if we don't, even we wouldn't be where we are. We would just be fighting all the time, you see? So we tried it to reconcile the people, and it was hard because you would find a family perished, maybe one person remained, all the others, some who perished completely, none at all. They [perpetrators] just come to the radio and talk and request for pardon...So, it was hard but the good* *thing also for the survivors of genocide; the government and even the population tried to at least be with them all the time. During the time of commemoration, we must be with them. You comfort them (Interview with the author, Kigali, 2013).*

The government, in particular, has not focused solely on rhetoric and moral support, but has tried to ease the material circumstances of genocide survivors, particularly orphans. *The government puts there some programs, support them. Like the children who survived, they pay their school fees, they gave them some small things, they constructed them houses, those who are sick they take them for treatment free of charge. There is a fund which was created where government puts in money, 5% of the national budget, and then also the community contributes, we even contribute from our salaries. But for the last 5 years they've stopped individual contributions, it is now the government because the number on the support is decreasing, because they learned, they come and work so they no longer need that support. ...Even in the rural areas, each one paid a certain amount to put in that fund....So people came to understand that the genocide was Rwandans against Rwandans. We also have to program ourselves. So we would pay that money comfortably. I think they were taking 15% of our yearly salaries...they put it into that fund. And the people paid it willingly, and the government put in something. So that's how we managed to reconcile...(Interview with the author, Kigali, 2013).* What is most striking about this type of program is that all Rwandans are contributing to the fund. It is not just the perpetrators, but everyone who has paid employment. This would include a whole spectrum of the society, such as those who were previously refugees and were not in the country or involved in the genocide. In this way, the whole society has been included in an aspect of the reconciliation process.

As another interviewee explained, *'So in Rwanda also, the genocide, first of all the genocide was also a result of a disintegration of the social fabric, because where the social fabric is strong there is no way a neighbour is going to go and hack down an entire family of neighbours. So, a lot is being done in terms reconciliation, in terms of this and that. But it is not something that can happen overnight (Interview with the author, Kigali, 2013).*

When asked if it was the extreme violence that has occurred in Rwanda's recent history that has created a sense of commitment to unity and equality, it was explained, *I hate to say it that way because I know people who keep saying 'Oh, Rwanda, oh all the progress it has made is because of the genocide', as if genocide is something we should all be looking for. No, I wouldn't like to say it that way, but I would like to say that when there is a movement for rights, you know, struggle for rights, then the people understand rights in its entirety. Which of course opens a window for women also because these are people who have*

93

struggled for rights, they understand what discrimination is, they understand what denial of rights is. But, I don't want to say because of our violent history because people have misused it, particularly in the case of Rwanda, to say 'oh, you know it is because of genocide then, you know, the country has,' no! It is not that. It is because of a better understanding of rights, you know? Indeed, the RPF especially, has had an inclusionary ideology from its founding outside of Rwanda, before the genocide. The RPF had already mainstreamed women into its political and armed structures before the war was over and they took over government (Debusscher & Ansoms 2013). Similarly, a South African woman emphasised that the point is not to address selected inequalities. *If you believe in equality then you've got to believe in equality, and above all, South Africans should know this given the way we've been divided (Interview with the author, Johannesburg, 2014).* In other words, it is the big picture of division and inequality, in Rwanda and South Africa, which inform political priorities. It is not the symptoms of divisions and inequalities (such as violence) that are necessarily the defining factor.

Conclusion

While according to US definitions of democracy, Rwanda is an authoritarian state, we have to interrogate whether this is the appropriate time to implement the western ideology of democracy. For Rwandans, democracy is about changing the society, about improving the quality of life of the people, providing them with employment, infrastructure, and security. It is argued that those outside of Rwanda who accuse it of authoritarianism are unaware of cultural peculiarities that are lost in translation; that only Rwandans are in a position to truly understand Rwanda (Herndon & Randell 2013). Indeed, we have to understand Rwandan history and experience from the Rwandan perspective to understand its politics.

In the South African context, some early childhood experiences represented the beginnings of a consciousness of three different kinds of inequalities; race, gender and class. Today, one of the causes of discord between women MPs and members of the women's movement is that they have different ideas of what it means to represent women. ANC women especially, are interested in the addressing all three forms of inequalities. They recognise that they are inter-related, and the various experiences cannot be neatly separated, boxed and labelled according to the three inequality categories, when you are, for example, a Black woman.

While here I discuss their experiences as an outsider, it becomes apparent that to understand their politics, it is necessary to look at women politicians through their own eyes, their own experiences, and how they have made meanings of those experiences, as much as is possible. Only then can we better understand who they are and what they bring to politics, as well as their challenges. It is additionally important to contextualise those experiences, which I attempt to do in the following chapters.

Chapter 5: Education as a Site of Oppression, Resistance and Survival

'But every woman has education; there's [no such thing as] a woman who is not educated...'

The majority of impoverished people around the world are women (Seager 2003). 60% of family workers around the world are women, but they earn 17% less than men. Also, girls are more likely to not be in school than boys (Goetz et al. 2009). Illiteracy is a problem for many reasons. Among them is that women are susceptible to having their votes influenced by men, thereby susceptible to voting against their own interests (Kantengwa 2010). Women are disproportionately represented amongst the illiterate around the world. Illiteracy is mostly a result of poverty and a lack of access to educational institutions. However, the higher rates of illiteracy amongst women indicate that that there is also a gender bias in education. Illiteracy for women is a huge problem because it impedes their ability to know and understand their rights (or lack of), it increases their dependency on men, it maintains their position in the domestic sphere, and limits their economic opportunities (Seager 2003). *I think one of the first things, especially with basic education; people don't know their rights. Most people don't know their rights. Most women in the urban informal settlement and rural areas don't know their rights; so we need to bridge that gap (Interview with author, Pretoria, 2014).*

In the literature on gender and politics, supply side factors with regards to political participation highlight the personal characteristics such as ambition, interest, knowledge, resources (like time and money), networks, skills, and education of women politicians. These are the factors that determine their suitability and availability for political office. In other words, the supply or availability of women for political leadership is affected by gender socialisation, which largely impacts their interest, ambition, skills and knowledge (Kunovich et al. 2007).

In the Global North, education has been found to be an indicator of women's representation because it makes more women interested in politics and competing in elections, as well as giving them the necessary skills to do so. Gender and education levels are an explanation for the varying political participation between women and men, with men more likely to participate in politics in various ways. In Sub-Saharan Africa the education gender gap is high. That being said, cross-nationally there hasn't been enough evidence to support the idea that education levels can predict political participation. Similarly, women in the wage labour force are the most politically active because they experience a confidence boost and some independence from men. The skills gained in the work force are invaluable, such as being able to supervise others. However, in Sub-Saharan Africa women's employment in the formal sector is low; most are in the informal or agricultural sectors. In this case, it is found that women's access to education and participation in the labour force are not determinants of women's representation, as they are in industrialised countries (Kunovich et al. 2007; Yoon 2004).

This chapter explores the educational qualifications and professional experience of women in politics in Rwanda and South Africa. However, I try to more than just aggregate education and professional experience as indicators of political participation. Rather, I try to contextualise the experiences of the women interviewed in the societies that they come from, in an attempt to not only understand what skills and expertise they bring to politics, but how they compare to ordinary women. I find that education and work experience is indeed important, but not in ways one might expect. Education does not only provide the skills required for political office. Rather, education and early professional experience appear to lead to their entry into politics, by contributing to their political and social awareness. *I think education - education is critical. There is no other way I can put it. Because education does so much. So much for you. I don't think any of us would be in positions we are in, we'd be doing work we are doing, if we had been denied education, and that's one thing I really appreciate about our parents (Interview with author, Kigali, 2013).*

Why is Education Important and why do Girls have Limited Access?

Many studies have shown that low levels of education can contribute to a conflict risk. In a study of 47, out of 63, civil wars between 1965 and 1999 conflict occurred predominantly in countries with poor educational levels. A 10% increase in education reduces the risk of conflict by between 10% and 14%. In addition, countries with a large male youth with low levels of secondary schooling are at a higher risk of conflict. This risk is exacerbated by unequal access to education. For example, there is a link between educational discrimination of on non-elite, rural, indigenous people, and armed rebellion. The type of education also plays a role; curriculum can be created and used to further political agendas. On the other hand, education can be a tool to prevent conflict – by improving access and teaching conflict resolution skills (McLean Hilker 2011). In countries such as Rwanda and South Africa, where conflict remains a recent memory, it becomes even more important to eliminate conditions that may foster renewed tensions, such low education levels.

The education of women and girls is not only important for creating a pool of qualified women for politics. Educating girls is shown to be important for the betterment of all of society. Educated women are more likely to have smaller families, be healthy, and have healthy and educated children (Girls' Education Movement n.d.). Unfortunately, in many African countries, parents have higher expectations for boys than girls. Daughters are married into other families who would benefit from their education, whereas boys would contribute to the family that invested in them. This is one of the biggest causes of low enrolment and high dropout rates for girls (Martineau 1997). This discriminatory practice of prioritising boys education over girls has been the case in Rwanda. *Our background says that women were not kept at school, they would [stay] at home to help their mothers and the chance to study was for boys. So for the first time we need these 30% [quotas] but, as we have this policy of equal rights to study I think with time we'll cancel this 30% and compete because we will be at the same level to compete (Interview with the author, Kigali, 2013).* Here she is referring to the 30% gender quotas that Rwanda has. She is making the argument that the quotas are necessary because of the uneven educational levels between women and men. Once women and men are educated equally, they would be better able to compete for political positions on an even playing field.

South Africa also has a history of educational inequalities based on gender. *You see that someone will after all get married, and so you don't need to invest too much money into her education because it's education that will not add value to her family; she's going to go to another home. So there are these very deep-seated attitudes on this person called a woman; after all she's going to be spending the greater part of her life as a mother and as a wife and cleaning the house (Interview with the author, Pretoria, 2014).*

It is within this cultural bias to educate boys that the women I interviewed grew up in. Interestingly, they all had at least undergraduate degrees, and the majority had postgraduate degrees. Their educational journeys are discussed in more detail below. However, it indicates that while education levels are not an indication of women's political participation in Sub-Saharan Africa, it does not mean that women in politics are necessarily uneducated.

The issue of educating girls and women is not only a necessity to better society, but it is also an issue of women's rights. *Education ...will reduce the risk* of you being a victim of any sort. Let's even talk about violence against women and girls...you are much less likely to be a victim of violence if you are educated and you have been empowered... as a person. First of all you will be able to protect yourself, keep away from circumstances that might expose you to that violence, secondly you won't be, like a lot of young girls, disadvantaged young girls. They can be attracted by people with a little money, give them little gifts and so on and so forth. I am currently carrying out a study on violence against adolescent girls in Rwanda. And, what we are finding is that most of the victims of violence, they dropped out of school at a certain time, maybe because of poverty, ignorance, all kinds of things. But when you see the cycle of violence that follows them after that, because we are carrying it out on the girls who are out of school and the ones who are still in school. You know the difference is enormous. So education is going to allow you to have a career and live a decent life. Education is going to allow you to go into political leadership if that is what you want to do. Education is going to enable you to understand life, to make reasonable choices about your life. I don't know what would really be...higher in terms of priority than education. I think it's because even if you say health, education also is most likely to improve your health status because you even know about seeking medical attention when you need it. And studies have been carried out, they even show, that you know, families where the mothers are educated, even if it is basic education, the status health, economic, social of the home is much better (Interview with the author, Kigali, 2013).

The Politics of Education

Besides the gendered inequalities in access to education, Rwanda and South Africa have a history of unequal access to education on the basis of race and ethnicity as well. Until 1948 missionary schools were the norm for African students in South Africa. In terms of girls' education, the mission schools were more interested in creating domestically skilled Christian wives for the male African elite who worked as teachers and preachers, rather than giving girls training or academic educations. After 1948, and the National Party (NP) came to power, the government took control of African students' education. In 1953 the Bantu Education Act was passed, which linked tax receipts from Blacks to public spending on their education. Spending on white education was 15 times more than on Black education at one point. Spending on education reflected the inequalities that existed amongst all the racial groups. For example, in 1989 ZAR4 was spent on every white child for ZAR1 for each black child. For coloured it was ZAR2 and for Asians ZAR3. In 1991 more than half of white men had completed high school, whereas only one in 12 black men had completed high school. The primary school syllabus for African students was designed to provide only basic mathematics and communication skills, and stressed obedience and acceptance of social roles. In essence, African students were only being trained to work in service for the white population. During Apartheid education was separate and unequal (Martineau 1997; Thomas 1996).

Rwanda's colonial educational institutions served the same purpose as the missionary schools in South Africa, particularly in the education of girls. Rwanda was a patriarchal society before colonialism, but this was exacerbated by unequal access to education when the formal education system was introduced. Women were only allowed to enter school forty years after men, and even then it was to train them to be perfect wives to colonial administration assistants (Kantengwa 2010). During the German and Belgian colonisation of Rwanda, Catholic missionary schools constituted the formal education system. These schools also provided basic education and trained Black clergy and colonial administrators for Belgian indirect rule. In addition, post-primary education was largely limited to the favoured Tutsi. Girls were not taught skills, but were trained in domestic tasks, to be good Christian wives for the colonial administrators, and to raise the next generation of African servants for the Belgian colony (McLean Hilker 2011; Ricketts 2013).

After Independence in 1962 the Hutu leadership wanted to end the economic and political dominance of the Tutsi and educate more Hutu. While the then government included in its constitution that primary education would be free and mandatory, it still remained unequal in access based on class, ethnicity and region. Primary school access did improve, however, there were limited opportunities for a secondary education, due to limited space and high costs – meaning that secondary and tertiary education was for the elite (McLean Hilker 2011).Under the Second Hutu Republic there was a new law that controlled access to education by several criteria; exam results, gender, ethnic and regional quotas, amongst others. These criteria were then used to discriminate against Tutsi students. For example, Tutsi quotas were lower than their population level. In 1898/90 there were 7.4% Tutsi and 91.4% Hutu students in grade 1. The trend was the same in secondary and tertiary institutions. In two provinces in 1981-1982 only 23% of Tutsi students who had passed their exams made it to tertiary institutions (McLean Hilker 2011).

However, most of the Rwandan women interviewed here did not attend primary and secondary school in Rwanda, except for one. One received her education in the Democratic Republic of the Congo, and four received their primary and secondary educations in Uganda. While they were not subject to the educational inequalities that existed in Rwanda, they did grow up in difficult circumstances as refugees. *We grew up in, some in refugee camps, some in different circumstances. Life was not easy. But most of our parents; the thing they wanted most was the education of their children. They'd rather go and do all the work, very few would take their children out of school to help, and they needed the help, they needed the labour, you know? You're thrown there without any possessions, without anything, but really I appreciate this and I really keep saying I hope it gets heard. Our parents were unbelievable because they would spare nothing to make sure that we were educated (Interview with the author, Kigali, 2013).* In other words, while they did not experience the educational inequalities in Rwanda at the time, their educational journey was no less difficult.

Another Rwandan participant expressed the importance of the determination of her mother, which enabled her to receive an education. *I told you in 1963 my mother ran away from Rwanda as a refugee with my sister and brothers. That was after my father was killed at the end of 1962. So she became a widow with children and my mother said, I used to hear her telling other women that, 'my children must go to school'. So I think the fact that my mother in the early 60's decided to send me to school, despite her challenging environment as a refugee widow, without any property, with working from hand to mouth, you know? But she decided to send me to school instead of me helping her, I think that became the departing point, the point of departure, you know? Because there are many young girls of my age, very intelligent, very capable, whose parents did not put in a lot of effort, probably they did not put in an effort, or there were other factors, I don't know. But I know my mother said, 'she must go to school' (Interview with the author, Kigali, 2013).* Both stories illustrate that everyone's contribution was needed for survival as refugees, however, these parents were willing to forego the assistance of their children to ensure that they might have better opportunities in future.

In addition to the will and sacrifice of parents, there were other support structures that enabled them to receive educations, as the same women explained. *So I went to school, and it was a village, poor school, but there were also teachers who were in those schools, some of them relatives, others neighbours, who really were interested in us, despite the fact that the school environment was poor, but they were very interested in us and encouraging. I always remember some of the teachers who were really encouraging us (Interview with the author, Kigali, 2013).* While the schools lacked material and infrastructure resources, the human resources was what made it possible for these refugee children to be educated. One anecdote illustrates the importance of the teachers, particularly. *So when I reached high school I met this lady, Doreen Drake, who was a British missionary and she helped both financially, but also mentoring us. And she was the type of woman we feared, you know as young people you must have somebody you have to fear so that you can read, and you pass your exams and all that because my mum didn't know, she couldn't know the chemistry I was reading, she couldn't know the biology I was reading, so I think this one came in as a godsend mentor because she would say, 'you must work hard, you know you come from poor families, you must graduate' (Interview with the author, Kigali, 2013).*

Perhaps what is most striking in this story is the sheer determination of a mother in the most dire circumstances, but also, a sacrifice of overlooking immediate comfort for future security. This story indicates a collective will by numerous people, parents, teachers, neighbours, etc., who wanted to ensure better circumstances for their children. Perhaps it was the unstable, insecure conditions and prospects for the future that forced refugee families to disregard gendered norms for access to education, which were continuing in Rwanda. *So my mother had said that, 'my daughter goes to school so that she can read sign posts.' Because when she was running as a refugee from Rwanda to Uganda she would pass by sign posts, but there were not many, but she couldn't read them. So she said, 'my children must learn how to read so that they can read signs so that when they travel'...she could see that now getting out of Rwanda, she didn't know when we'd come back, she could see that we were going to move from place to place, from country to country, and reading was a tool that would facilitate that aspect (Interview with the author, Kigali, 2013).* In other words, education was not simply a means of attaining a better quality of life in the future, but also a tool for survival during uncertain times.

That is not to say that difficult and unstable circumstances are always the reason for educating girls. One woman, who grew up in Rwanda, also had the determination of a parent to ensure that she was educated. *Someone who encouraged me first of all was my father. But it was a long time ago because he died in 1994 genocide. But while I was still young, as a girl, actually I think I was brilliant because my father was proud of me. And I know he was always supportive and he was sometimes giving examples, taking me as a model in the family. In addition to telling my brothers, 'yeah, so why don't you do like her?' Or 'Why don't you do like this?' And I was young compared to my brothers...we were two girls out of eight children, others were boys. And me especially because I was young, the youngest girl at home, he was always referring to me as a model, he was encouraging me to go beyond (Interview with the author, Kigali,*

2013). Similarly to those who had left the country, the community also played an important role in her education. *[I was] very intelligent, very brilliant at school...I studied in schools led by missionaries from Europe, and their education was right for girls, and I was lucky when I reached the school the first year, I secured the first position in the school. And everybody was attentive; the headmaster, the professors encouraged me, and they encouraged me to push (Interview with the author, Kigali, 2013).* While missionary schools and gendered discrimination in access (as discussed earlier), were structural problems in Rwanda's education system, this interviewees story illustrates that there were exceptions. Her story is exceptional because her experience went against the norm; she attended a school that encouraged her progress despite the fact that she was a girl, and her family did not treat her unequally because she was a girl (in fact she was favoured because of her intelligence). Rather than disadvantage her because of the mere fact of her being born a girl, she was supported and encouraged to excel in school.

These stories illustrate that while there was a general discrimination in terms of girls education, there were exceptions, for various reasons, such as the difficult refugee life creating a sense of urgency for education, the will of the parents, the recognition of the girl child's potential, or a combination of two or three of these factors. Of the women I interviewed in Rwanda, all had undergraduate degrees, and most had graduate degrees (except one who had actually begun studying for an MBA during the time of our interview). In this regard, Rwandan women politicians have higher levels of formal education than many of their peers around the world. The women surveyed in the IPU study were mostly well educated, with 73% having an undergraduate degree, 14% having postgraduate degrees, 7% had a high school diploma, and 6% had tertiary training (Waring et al 2000). Similarly, all but one of the South African women had postgraduate degrees.

Amongst the South African women interviewed, one also expressed the will and commitment of her mother to ensure that her daughters receive formal education. *Also she always wanted to go to study. She's one of 14 children and she was very clever but she wasn't allowed to study. There was only two out of the 14, and the two were men who went to university and therefore she lived, I think her thoughts, ambitions, through the daughters – everyone going to university subsequently (Interview with the author, Kigali, 2013).* In other words, in both the Rwandan and South African examples of the mothers' commitment to educating their children; out of the mothers' own lack of education arose a determination to ensure that their children would be educated, and thereby spared the difficulties and unfairness that they had experienced, respectively.

Unlike the Rwandan women who spent most of their childhood outside of

Rwanda, the majority of the South African women interviewed here only left the country later in life, except for one. Therefore, their educational experiences were very much affected by the inequalities that existed within the country, and played a role in their awareness of the inequalities. *My father died very early and...as a black child, if the breadwinner dies you actually go and work, you don't go to school. And the family all said, 'oh, those girls must go to work'. My mother said, 'No, all my daughters will have professions.' And she just worked and we actually had to study. Even though we had part-time jobs; I remember cleaning the convent, these long corridors and dormitories and working until five in the morning at restaurants. One of the horrible jobs was a clothing store...But also it made you a richer person. I actually saw the race hierarchy and the hierarchy of working: the way you were treated, the way you were spoken to in front of customers – [it made me] even more determined that I must change this country, I must be educated, I must go to university – by your sheer experience (Interview with the author, Kigali, 2013).* In this story we see the intersection between race and gender. As she explained, when the breadwinner dies the Black children have to work to supplement the household income. In addition, she came from a family (as she explained earlier) where girls' education was not a priority, which subsequently changed within her nuclear family through the determination of her mother. These circumstances also led to her working and experiencing the treatment of those who worked in service for white people who subscribed to the Apartheid hierarchy. Here there are the triple inequalities of gender, race and class.

Despite the unequal and poor education system during Apartheid, enrolment rates were different from those in other African countries. By 1955 girls' enrolment in primary school matched those of boys. However, not many women went on to complete secondary schooling. For example, in 1985 less than 5% of Black women had completed secondary school. In addition, males and females were pushed in different directions; more boys were trained while girls were prepared for domestic work. The lack of access and poor quality of education for Black women meant that many were uneducated and unskilled, and had to work as domestic workers, prostitutes and beer brewers (Martineau 1997).

Between 1960 and 1985 illiteracy rates for Indian and Coloured women fell, but illiteracy rates for African women remained above 50%. However, in 1985 44% of students in tertiary institutions where women, but many of them were enrolled in long-distance correspondence programs (Martineau 1997). *I did part of my matric in Morris Isaacson but I didn't complete because I had to leave school and go and work. So I corresponded with the long distance education facilitated by Damelin College. So I wrote my matric with Damelin (Interview with the author, Pretoria, 2014, TM).* Matric is the final year of high school in South Africa. This interviewee's story shows that correspondence was not just a solution for tertiary education, but also for those who wanted to complete high school but couldn't do so in traditional high school institutions. However, this story also shows that education was not only segregated by race, but was also affected by class, by the fact that she couldn't continue as a normal high school student, but had to work as a teenager, similarly to the previous anecdote.

While the educational institutions were separated under Apartheid, one participant was able to attend a non-black University, but had to receive permission in the form of pass. *I chose to go to go university, I chose to go to UCT and it was also problematic, like I had to have a pass, I had to have a permit for UCT (Interview with the author, Kigali, 2013).* Similarly, the subjects that were available to Black people were restricted. *I studied science first and then I was not able to complete because I allergic to certain chemicals. So then by that time I was also much more aware of what I wanted to do with myself and that I wanted to come back to South Africa. And there wasn't much that any black could do except become a doctor or a lawyer or a teacher, or something like that. So I decided, no, I'd rather be a lawyer – that's how it happened. I found the science education interesting and very useful to me but I couldn't do it as a profession because I knew there was nothing I could have done (Interview with the author, Johannesburg, 2014).* This participant was partly educated in England, and amongst South Africa's political leadership, foreign qualifications are not exceptional. In the 1980's there were about 1500 ANC members receiving tertiary educations in American, European and British universities, which was a substantial figure. Communist countries provided more technical educations to ANC members (Lodge 1987).

In addition, while career options for Black people were limited, women were doubly disadvantaged in career prospects. Women were overwhelmingly enrolled in socially feminine caretaker courses such as nursing and teaching (Martineau 1997). *And then I went back to boarding school and I went to school like everybody else and I qualified as a teacher, which was not something I had really planned but the opportunities in those days because of apartheid and discrimination and the limitation of funds – my parents couldn't send all of us because boarding school was very expensive for all of us at home. Then we all had to go to secondary school in boarding school and go to high school. So parents couldn't afford to send all of us; so I never had an opportunity to go to university then. I was then trained as a teacher. And a year after I had been a teacher I was lucky to get a scholarship and be trained again as a social worker. And then later on I got opportunities, I continued with my studies [indistinct] management and then I was lucky later to go to the United States in the later years. But a long journey, I finally got my master's degree in communication (Interview with the author, Pretoria, 2014).* In the same way that this woman was constrained by costs of education, another interviewee was limited in her options because her parents too, could not afford to pay university fees. *After finishing matric I actually did a secretarial course, largely because my parents couldn't afford taking all of us to post-matric degree level; so we took different options and then thereafter I did some diplomas, one in journalism, in personnel and training (Interview with the author, Pretoria, 2014).* Again, the class inequalities of that time determined one's access to higher education, and also what type of education if one could afford to go to a tertiary institution.

In South Africa the education system was not only a site in which inequalities were cemented by the Apartheid regime through race and class, they also became sites of resistance. In 1976 the Soweto Riots took place; school children protested against Bantu education, and the Apartheid police responded with violence by shooting them, which resulted in many deaths. However, school boycotts continued right through the 1980's (Thomas 1996). The Soweto Uprising of 1976, in particular, can be viewed as the reawakening of political consciousness of South Africa (Lodge 1987). However, as this participant's story shows; the struggle against the education system in particular was not concentrated in the streets of Soweto, *As a student I was an activist, I was a member of COSAS ...So in terms of a political career and activism, it started in the very early 1970s when I was still at high school (Interview with the author, Pretoria, 2014).*

COSAS (The Congress of South African Students) was a national organisation founded in 1979 to represent the interests of Black South African students after the Soweto Uprisings. It included high school students and students at tertiary institutions. COSAS was against the Bantu Education system, and had the view that the education system could only be equal within an equal society. While representing students' concerns and fighting against the unequal education system, it was essentially an Anti-Apartheid movement (South African History Online 2015).

It appears that for many of those interviewed, activism against Apartheid started early in life, as school children. *I was always politically involved. At high school using drama in the form of politics and politicising people, using drama, going to orphanages, playing at old-age homes and different places with theatre. So it was just inevitable that I was going to be involved in politics (Interview with the author, Kigali, 2013).*

Not only were there various student activities and boycotts, some special schools also served as sites of resistance as well. *Ohlange High School is a school*

106

that was built by John Langalibalele Dube and Nokutela, his first wife. And what used to happen because his house was not far away from school, so at the beginning of the year, the first weekend we had to all go to his home. His second wife, Angelina Dube, was still alive even though she was on a wheelchair at the time – so we would all go there from one from Form 1 to Form 5 – Form 1 now it's called Grade 7! So we had to go there, sit on the lawn and she would sit on the veranda and she would ask us to sing…So she would talk to us. And then in the midst of that she would tell us about the stories of her husband, she's involved maybe in the ANC; the consequences of those choices for their family, and then he died. But also starting to explain the motivation behind the building of the school, that it was really a form of struggle to empower black children who otherwise wouldn't have had an opportunity for education; so that was the real issue that made him to think of the idea of a school so that no black child would actually not have an opportunity of studying.

Outside of South Africa during exile, an ANC educational institution, the Department of Education and Culture, was located in Morogoro, Tanzania. After the Soweto riots and the influx of new, young, revolutionaries from South Africa, the ANC recognised the need to provide secondary education when it received these school children. The Department began with just 80 students, but had had grown to 1000 students in 1983. The instruction was not only traditional curriculum, but included skills required for governance, and emphasised social and political principles (Lodge 1987). In the MK camps the soldiers in training received military and political education (Curnow 2000).

Political activism while at higher education institutions provided women with networks to become involved in national politics. In the experiences of some women MPs around the world, the tertiary institution was a site of becoming aware of the need to use politics for redress of inequality and injustice. The inequalities and injustices identified vary from the inequalities for indigenous people, inequalities for women in all sectors of society, to the plight of children. In some cases, women spoke of very specific issues, such as poor formal education, corruption, or women's low literacy (Waring et al. 2000). *And then after corresponding I went to Fort Hare and by that time I was quite old because I was now 22-23. The first year there was as strike and the strike was a solidarity strike about Onkgopotse Tiro and Turfloop. Where Onkgopotse was graduating but his parents could not come and sit in the front. It was the relatives of all the teaching staff and the white staff of Turfloop, and the Turfloop students then took this up as to how can a person be graduating and instead the people who enjoy the occasion are the White people. And then there were solidarity strikes. And I was at Fort Hare. But at Fort Hare not only did we stop at solidarity strikes, we extended it to conditions at Fort Hare and we ended up extending it to Bantu education. So I was kicked out of Fort Hare, and that was my first year and my only time that I had opportunity (Interview with the author, Pretoria, 2014).* In a country in which women and black people were already largely excluded from educational institutions, this participant sacrificed her education for her people, because of the injustices that they were experiencing, which indicates a deep commitment to changing her society.

By that time I was in SASO, a busy black student organisation at that time led by Steve Biko. So when I got kicked out I didn't really go home; I remained in the Eastern Cape. First we had what was called the Student's Action Committee. We went around the country explaining why we were on strike, calling student-parent meetings and explaining ourselves...We formed something of a commune because then we started having black community programmes and then we had Black People's Conventions and we had Dumela Trust Fund – all the things that we could do around Black Consciousness to say, 'black person you are on your own, you must do things your way'. And then interpreting apartheid and interpreting what black people have to do in terms of freeing themselves – that's the most critical part of your consciousness. That was the Black Consciousness of that time. So those are my formative years. Her activism subsequently led to her imprisonment by the Apartheid police. *But then between 1976 and 1977 I get arrested more than eight times under different laws – the Section 6, Section 22, Section 10 – all these laws. And my comrades of that time feel that I'm likely to be killed as the rate things are going. By that [time] we need to go and start the Black Consciousness Movement outside anyway (Interview with the author, Pretoria, 2014).*

While the 1970's and 1980's were the biggest years in terms of student activism, as illustrated above, students were active much earlier than that. *But I started to be in the struggle as a school girl at Lovedale where I went to do my primary higher teaching certificate. And in 1952 it was a great year of the Defiance Campaign and we were all over, and everybody was being affected and so a number of us at the girls' school had joined the Defiance Campaign. I don't think we knew exactly what it was anyway! And there used to be young men who would come from Fort Hare to come and give us a report and the plans what to do. So I was part of the group in 1953; rather young at the time but of course when you are young you think you are not young, and we were organising that we are going to defy and go to a cafe that was a very famous cafe, Ramona Cafe in Alex...And you know what we're going to do? We were going to occupy the white access, walk into this cafeteria and sit in the cafeteria we were not allowed to occupy. And then we were also going to go at the station – I mean, really, this was a great act...go to the station and we're going to go to the trains that had compartments for whites.*

While education was separate and unequal, and educational institutions became sites of violence, they also became sites of resistance, of consciousness raising, and political networking, as illustrated in the narratives above. Besides the traditional education system, some South Africans received a special kind of education; a political education. *I think that's lacking now in the Youth League, is that we had political education all the time. I think it was a particular moment that also demanded that we understand where we're going to and what we want, how do we struggle, how do you strategise, how do we strategise? What's worked or doesn't work? So it was politically very inspiring and there were amazing people like Dorothy Zihlangu, Dorothy Mfaco, Mildred Lesiea. And we always say, gosh, we went to university but Lynne Brown and I were very close and quite a lot we would say that those are our political leaders, these are women who were domestic workers but they were the leaders in the organisations and we promoted working class leadership. And even though they could not analyse politically with the jargon that we used, they still could understand everything – it was really very, very, very inspiring. (Interview with the author, Kigali, 2013).* This highlights a very important point; that just because women (or an individual) have not attended university, does not mean that they are not aware of the complexities of the issues that plague society. Perhaps the barrier is the technical language, but the awareness and passion was there. In other words, a lack of a traditional education should not form a barrier to political leadership. However, once in leadership, not having received traditional schooling can become an obstacle.

Other Ways of Thinking about Education

In South Africa, men and women MPs struggled with the nature of parliament in terms of the strong legal language, having to read and understand countless reports, having no experience with parliamentary procedures, an intense workload, and a lack of immediacy in results (Geisler 2000). Geisler (2000: 617) quotes a woman MP who could not believe that she was elected to parliament because she was not 'well educated'. Another woman MP was shocked to have moved from a township teaching job to a parliamentary seat (Geisler 2000). *And I think for me that story is always a very important story of how grassroots women*

– when Lydia Kompe was the founder of the, at that time it was Transvaal Women's Rural Action Movement, and she was in parliament. At the first interview she said, 'I'm just an ordinary woman, I'm not quite sure why; I can't read.' Every day you get to your desk and you've got a pile of documents that you've got to read. And that's all you read and it's just way beyond people. I struggled, even though I have tertiary education, to get through all the documentation. And she said, 'What am I doing here? What is my role here?' (Interview with the author, Kigali, 2013).

The question then becomes how can we ensure that those women (and men) who are disadvantaged in educational opportunities are not excluded from leadership and decision-making positions? Also, how can we ensure that once they are in these positions they do not become demoralised by the difficulty of the work? The South African case in particular indicates that in some ways the Western emphasis on diplomas and degrees should not dominate our ideas about competence and skills, especially in countries such as Rwanda and South Africa where the historical conditions prevented many from receiving educations. A Rwandan participant explained that there are other ways to receive an 'education'.

...My big inspiration is my context. As a Rwandese, being sensitive on women issues, this is because even our life as women of Rwanda is like a book. You don't need to go and read a book written by an expert somewhere; you can read through your context, through your life and through another woman's life. That is the book I am reading every day...because I cannot quote the book I've read in schools, in universities, the ones I'm reading today. I'm more and more inspired by the experience of others, my own life, the lives of my fellow women are a book (Interview with the author, Kigali, 2013).

This is not to say that formal education is not important. However, in societies where groups have been discriminated against in educational opportunities, education should not act as exclusionary mechanism to further marginalise those who have not received adequate educations (however we might measure that); *When we started to train women councillors it was tough because some of these women had never been in any movement in their life, and some of them didn't have much formal education. But every woman has education; there's [no such things as] a woman who is not educated – anyone who can run a home and budget for a home, I can tell you, can run and be a councillor once she's given this (Interview with the author, Pretoria, 2013).* This statement illustrates that women's experiences are under-valued, and that even women who have only worked in the domestic sphere do have skills that can be transferred to the public sphere.

There are some ways to bridge the gap between experience and formal education, and innovative solutions can be found. *The first three months I mobilised a cohort of young scientists and social scientists, economists, and every night I would meet with them just to take me through. But what was good was that the majority of those came from the liberation movement, so I could talk the politics of agriculture and its role in society and its role in the economy. And for me agriculture, my basic knowledge was about planting, then harvesting and eating. But to understand how intricate the economy and the roles that the sector played in there – wow! So it meant beyond reading I also had to be vigilant so I can go to any meeting and [not] only be confrontational on what my memo says; I also had to look out what the others say because that has a consequence on my ministry. For instance, some decisions that could be taken about trade and production…If the scarcity of water is not balanced between farmers and people, it's only given to people and farmers are then not productive – so you started to link these things. But that also meant you had to read more (Interview with the author, Pretoria, 2014).* In other words, self-education and enlisting the help of those who have received formal training can be a strategy to close the gap between experience and knowledge.

In addition, education should be a continuing process that addresses the particular areas in which women may be lacking. *And we've got to have some skills, equipment for women, even to talk to the media. Because we have not been as exposed as men in our lives, you just don't know how to handle media; even to talk in parliament you just don't know. Men need this training too but particularly women and particularly women who came in through the quota system – because you are empowering them now. This is to make sure that not only do they access, enter parliament, but they participate (Interview with the author, Pretoria, 2014).* Particularly when there are concerns that women who come in through quotas are just tokens, and therefore are not capable, special trainings and education programs can provide a boost.

Additionally, increasing women's representation is not only about increasing numbers, as this interviewee explains and has been discussed previously. Rather, it should be about empowering women, those elected and those that they represent. *At some point I did my own research and I found that in fact the participation of women in debates, according to what I found…participation of women was about 30%, but raising gender-related issues was about 10%. So the assumption that once you have accessed parliament then we have the happy ever after is a wrong one…quotas facilitate the entry but they don't assist in participation. So the empowerment assists in the participation. But it's not just participation, it's what kind and how do you engender policies? How do you engender parliament? How do you make it a point that everything is transformed so these women not only participate but assist and transform parliament; they transform the institution itself, which we did when we got in by having even child-care facilities because the sessions were long and you didn't have a child-care facility (Interview with the author, Pretoria, 2014).* In other words, the exercise of increasing women's representation is not about empowering those few women who make it to parliament, but it is necessary to empower them to also represent the interests of women; empower the representatives to empower the citizens.

In and of itself the institution of parliament itself is informative and a learning experience. *So by joining the parliament, by being a politician you get a lot of experiences. First of all with the community work...working for your country...being in a refugee situation for all those years and coming back, so it was positive, I liked it. Secondly, travelling, I think I first travelled when I was going for education in Zambia, I'd never gone abroad, but when I joined the parliament I went to different places in Africa and Europe, in Asia, in America, so I got various experiences, sharing with people, so you get to know how things are done. The politics of other countries, you share with fellow women, you find even in other places women are struggling to get their numbers we have in Rwanda (Interview with the author, Kigali, 2013).* This interviewee explains that the parliament itself becomes a learning experience, but other women in other countries can become resources as well. Women can advise each other on what has or has not worked for them, which would provide another form of training.

Furthermore, more experienced women can provide special trainings in specific areas to newer women. *I've just come from an interesting group of women. These women are being trained; they are going to be ambassadors and high commissioners. And they are not only South Africans but they are also coming from other countries in Africa. And one of the areas they are focusing on is women mediators. There are many, many organisations in the continent of Africa who do mediation work. Some of this mediation work is of different kinds; we've had all kinds of conflicts in the continent. We have the current ones and then the old ones. Sudan has been in the list for a long, long time and then you have had now the two Sudans...then there are more problems. Then you have Mali, then you have Egypt – so it's a lot of these countries in the continent. And Mozambique is coming on. Then you have Tunisia; then there's Libya, and so on and so forth. But most of these countries you find they have a lot of men, although the UN and the African Union made a decision a long time ago that they should include women – but it's not working. And you find that these people who are signing all these agreements will be mostly male. And then people who go out to countries...I will be giving lectures to them later on in two areas; generally on the women and mediation and then the second part will be specifically on mediation for elections...(Interview with the author, Pretoria, 2014).* In other words, context-specific education and training can be another way of improving the skills of women in politics. In this case, women are receiving training to both be able to handle the unique issues plaguing the African continent, but also to be able to represent women's interests in peace processes, something that Rwandan and South African women have done successfully. Furthermore, women should not only be a resource for each other cross-nationally, but also in terms of more experienced women providing training for those that are just starting out.

Creating a New Generation of Competent Leadership

Despite encouraging developments such as this, there remain challenges in education. South Africa has received huge inequalities in education from the Apartheid government. In a democratic South Africa the tertiary system faces the challenge of creating equality in access, resources, output and employment (Martineau 1997; Hoogeveen & Ozler 2007). *Because our school system is deplorable. Why? If you look at what Bantu education did, coloured education, Indian education, it was all separate curriculum. And no research, no broadening of the mind – so there you are (Interview with the author, Johannesburg, 2014).* Besides for needing to make the education system equal, it faces numerous other challenges. These include poor quality, poor infrastructure and sanitation, students from poor homes going hungry, and low teacher morale. Girls are especially vulnerable as they are not safe from sexual assaults and harassments in the schools (Girls' Education Movement n.d.).

Rwanda also faces its own challenges. More women are enrolling in university, but illiteracy rates are still high; rates for women are 58.1% for men and 47.8% for women. There is also a gender inequality in access. Men are also more likely to receive training and education. 17% of men have never attended school, while 25% of women have never been to school. These gender differences are even larger in the rural areas where most women are living (Uwineza & Pearson 2009).

Unlike South Africa, which has to transform the education system, Rwanda was not only faced with transforming the curriculum and the system, but had to restart from almost nothing. Rwanda's school infrastructure and human resources were destroyed by the genocide. As much as 75% of teachers were killed or in jail for participating in the genocide. 70% of children were traumatised from witnessing the violence and death in the genocide. Exposed children are said to finish half a year less of schooling than other children. Rwanda also has high repetition and drop-out rates. However, the government has done a great deal in improving access to education. It has a policy of free basic education from the ages of 6 to 9 years. Primary enrolment rates have drastically improved, increasing approximately 12% between 2000/2001 and 2005/2006. Completion rates have also improved. Enrolment rates at the secondary level have not improved as much (Kestelyn 2010; McLean Hilker 2011). *And we have this program, 'Education for All' so everybody can access to schools. We have the free education from the primary to secondary school. The government - free education for those who went in public schools, but if you go in private there you can pay something. But for government it is a free education (Interview with the author, Kigali, 2013).*

In addition, at the tertiary level the government has established new institutions; the result being that there was an increase in the number of students from 10 000 in 2002 to 27 787 in 2005 (Kestelyn 2010; McLean Hilker 2011).[9]

Rwanda has shown a commitment to girls' education in particular. In 2008 there was a net enrolment rate of 95.1% for girls and 93.3% for boys. While girls' enrolment at primary school is high, their access to the full education cycle is lower than boys. Girls' performance in the maths, sciences and technology subjects is poorer than boys' as well. Challenges for girls include sexual harassment, few female role models, discrimination against girls in the curriculum and teaching, poverty, not being able to afford menstruation products, and continued cultural preferences to educate boys (Kestelyn 2010). However, efforts are being made. *There is a lot that is being done for girls to keep being educated. Like there is the first lady's program, and a lot of other associations, even I can say there are many schools for girls; girl schools. So all those are encouraging girls to be educated (Interview with the author, Kigali, 2013).*

Ordinary Rwandans interviewed by Burnet (2011) felt that women's increased representation has led to girl's increased access to education. There are national campaigns to promote universal education, and educated women have access to careers and incomes, which has become an incentive for people to educate their daughters (Jennie E. Burnet, 2011).

---

[9] See McLean Hilker (2011) for a discussion for some of the challenges that face Rwanda's education system as well as remaining barriers to access.

Conclusion

Education is a powerful tool for women's empowerment, it improves their quality of life, it empowers them to be independent, and in general, a literate society with equal access to education is a more peaceful society. Access to education is mediated by numerous factors, such as poverty, ethnic/racial inequalities, and the gender bias of educating boys over girls, amongst others.

A commonality that Rwanda and South Africa share is how politicised education was prior to 1994. In Rwanda access to education was not only a class and gender issue, but also an ethnic issue controlled by different political powers at various times. The same can be said for South Africa, except that access was divided along racial lines, and there was also a special type of education; a political education as part of the consciousness raising in the Anti-Apartheid movement. Many such movements were involved, such as COSAS and the Black Consciousness Movement, and education was also available in exile.

While access to education within Rwanda was politicised, amongst refugee Rwandans it became an important means of survival. In such an environment, other priorities, such as labour and gendered biases were not as important.

Despite these difficult circumstances they grew up in, all of the women that I interviewed had at least an undergraduate degree, while all but two had post-graduate degrees during the times of the interviews. When viewed in relation to the education statistics of both countries, these women are a privileged few, particularly in Rwanda where illiteracy rates are still extremely high. However, when looking at the education of political leaders, as these women have shown, education does not have to become a candidacy criterion that automatically excludes competent, but formally uneducated women. Their experiences illustrate that in some contexts, the type of education can be more important than the type of institution in which it was obtained. Experience can also be a great teacher. However, going forward it is crucial that both countries improve the quality of the education systems, and improve access to education for a couple of reasons. Firstly, the more educated a society is, the lower the chance of violent conflict. Secondly, if gender equality in political representation is to be maintained then it is important to educate future generations.

The Rwandan and South African cases provide examples of why education levels are not an indicator of women's political participation in Sub-Saharan Africa. Interestingly, this does mean that women politicians in these countries are uneducated, though there are examples of this. Rather, that formal education has not been a barrier to access to leadership.

Chapter 6: Professional Careers, Activism and Entry into Politics

'And when if I have an opportunity to work for women I do it as a passion, not as a paid work but a passion.'

Across countries, there is a positive relationship between women's labour force participation and women's interest legislation (Kunovich et al. 2007). However, as indicated earlier, labour force participation is not an indicator of women's representation in Sub-Saharan Africa (Yoon 2004). Around the world, women are concentrated in the low-pay informal sector, such as domestic work and market selling (Seager 2003). Jobs are segregated into 'women's jobs' and 'men's jobs' (Seager 2003: 64). Women are concentrated not just in the informal sector, but in the services sector, and increasingly in the manufacturing assembly line (Seager 2003). Prior to 1994, Rwandan and South African women faced discrimination in the job market, partly owing to their low levels of educations (a result of the gender bias discussed above).

In Rwanda, after puberty women stayed in the home and participated in housework, and in the rural areas they participated in the cultivation of food crops. Only 19% of the private commercial sector included women in its labour force, and while there was more balance in the public sector, women held lower paying and ranking positions (Schindler 2009). In Rwanda, more women than men are part of the agricultural work force (Seager 2003). In Kigali, the capital, young urban women who were well educated and financially independent were sometimes harassed in public by police and soldiers. In one extreme case they were placed into detention centres and charged with prostitution (Schindler 2009).

Since the genocide, their situation has improved. Women's participation in associations, credit groups and farm cooperatives has risen. These groups serve as a replacement for the lost support networks and family ties due to the war (Schindler 2009).

In South Africa, the racial differences in profession and economic status caused by Apartheid are evidenced by 1995 government figures. These showed that Black women experience the highest level of unemployment. Most of those who were employed were domestic workers. Simultaneously, the racial division between women is stark; African women earned only 43% of what White women earned, and just 26% of what White men earned. Black women earned 89% of what Black men earned. This is an empirical example of the double-whammy of gender and race inequalities (Mtintso 2003). This figure shows that in 1995 at

116

least, Black women were economically more equal to Black men, than they were to White women. This is evidence of Mtintso's (2003) argument that sometimes other identities and experiences over-ride the gender identity. Things had not changed much by 1999. 52% of Black women were unemployed, as compared to 37% of Black men. 28% of Coloured women were unemployed, as compared to 19% of Coloured of men. 24% of Indian women were unemployed, as compared to 18% of Indian men. Lastly, 7% of White women were unemployed, as compared to 6% of White men (Seager 2003). These figures not only show that unemployment is disproportionately high amongst Black people, but the 15% unemployment difference between Black women and men shows that poverty is the domain of Black women. That there is only a 1% difference between White women and men, shows that unemployment challenges based on gender are disproportionately affecting Black women, as compared to White women.

Of course, the causes of this inequality can be traced back to Apartheid. In 1960 African women were about 7.5 million in population, but only 800 000 of them were considered to be economically active. 500 000 of them were working as domestic workers, 200 000 were labourers on white owned farms, 12 000 were nurses, 11 000 teachers, and the rest were factory workers (Martineau 1997). One South African interviewee was a member of the smaller group of trained professional women. *I was given a choice when I qualified as a social worker in South Africa. I had an offer of five jobs. The reason was that there were not many social workers who had been trained – that was the reason, it wasn't because it's me, it was because there was a demand for trained social workers. There were not enough people who were going for the course. And then there were some agencies who wanted women in particular and in my class when we graduated we were only two women and 10 men. So that's why then I had this choice with the jobs (Interview with the author, Pretoria, 2014).*

She explained that she first began working with women through her professional training, *…Then I had been working in Alexandra township which had…, for those days, a wonderful multi-something centre. But this particular centre had social workers full-time. It had nurses who were doing the child care. Then it had sections in this huge centre where women would be taught cooking and handicraft – name it. And I liked this centre very much and I was fascinated by it, working in this centre as a student with all these different facets of it. And I then chose to go and work for a women's organisation (Interview with the author, Pretoria, 2014).* Her experience, working with women and women's social issues, before entering government, is a common thread amongst the women that I interviewed, as well as women politicians around the world.

A significant number of women MPs come from civil society backgrounds

(42% of 187 in 1999). The next common professions include teaching, journalism, medicine, nursing, social work and law. Social work, and in organisations such as NGOs, provided a political consciousness and also served as a route into politics (Waring et al. 2000).

Women MPs in Rwanda come from a variety of backgrounds, such as medicine, business, and teaching (Powley 2006). However, most come from civil society (Devlin & Elgie 2008; Uwineza & Pearson 2009). *I worked for government and non-governmental organisations...prior to joining the parliament I was the coordinator for an international NGO here in Rwanda...I joined parliament in 2003. But I had been with that NGO since 1996. It is very very interesting because all my life I had been working in developmental activities. I had never thought of joining politics, but then I would say that because I was a foreigner, I never got interested much. But when I reached Rwanda, because we were repatriated in 1994... So when I came, of course coming back to your country, I got interested. I got interested because immediately [when] I arrived I got a job, I worked with government, I was a coordinator for repatriation and settlement in a province from 1994 to 1995. Then in 1996 I joined that NGO, and during that process there were some electoral offices which I was getting. Like, I was president of the Women's Council in that province. So, that was not a job, I was just elected...it is unpaid (Interview with the author, Kigali, 2013).*

The NGO (non-governmental organisations) sector played a crucial role in the aftermath of the genocide. Rwanda's women's movement, especially, stepped in and played a leading role in rebuilding Rwanda after the war and genocide. Many women gained skills and experience in this sector, which prepared them for political life and government work (Debusscher & Ansoms 2013). *I think my background helped me to make a contribution in my new role...I had worked for [an] international NGO in Kenya, so I was so used to the rural life, because I worked in the rural life, the rural Kenya. So I mean all over our countries the needs are the same. The needs of women in the rural area are the same everywhere. I also had worked for about three years with an NGO here, and I had worked with UNHCR, so I knew, somehow I knew what the needs were of women, so again, as this appointment was big jump for me but was also a great opportunity to use the knowledge and skills I had to organise mobilise and to program for women (Interview with the author, Kigali, 2013).* In other words, grassroots work enables women to know the needs of the people once they enter politics.

Similarly, another Rwandan began her professional career in civil society. *Actually even when I was working with different projects, it was projects aiming at supporting women. My first project after my university was called 'Support to the Advancement of Women'. And, it was after the 1994 genocide against the Tutsis, different efforts [were put] in place to support women to recover during the emergency time, and supported by different international organisations, especially agencies. And I joined a ministry to implement a project helping women to lead the emergence, to lead the transition in the development field. It was to help women to recover, to be economically included, to have a kind of social economic inclusion...help women to contribute to their own development, economic development, self-empowerment...But for me working with women is helping the society, and I like it, I do it not as a job, but as a passion because I am a woman, I know, and I'm sensitive to the issue[s] affecting women...And when if I have an opportunity to work for women I do it as a passion, not as a paid work but a passion (Interview with the author, Kigali, 2013).*

It is interesting in both of these stories is that these women were involved in women's organisations particularly, before entering government. *When I was in Kenya I was working for an NGO. I was serving in rural development because my background of education is agriculture. So when I came back in 1995 I had this passion to work in development, so a few months later I worked for a local NGO. I was like a program coordinator for two years. And then I got a job with UNHCR, heading a project [working with women]. So in a way I was looking for a job but I was also looking for a job that was pertinent to my interests. So I liked working with women after the genocide. Actually, this project was supposed to help in their rehabilitation, reintegration, and getting them to be part and parcel of the reconciliation and reconstruction of the country (Interview with the author, Kigali, 2013).*

For other women, the route to politics did not start in civil society. Around the world, 78% of women MPs worked their way up in political parties, some of them having been recruited because of their accomplishments (Waring et al. 2000). One woman I spoke to had almost no work experience when she was recruited to government, but was recruited because of her educational achievement, having completed her graduate degree in Europe. *When I finished my school...the government recruited me... When the government found out about me and my skills at the time they were interested in recruiting me to government. The government of Rwanda has a deliberate approach of identifying Rwandans in the diaspora who can come and contribute to its development, because it wants to increase its skills. So I was one of those many that the government goes out and finds in the diaspora and brings them back to Rwanda to contribute to its development. That's how I was approached by the government and then [they] recruited me to the Rwandan government (Interview with the author, Kigali,*

2013). However, this example was the only one amongst all the women I had interviewed. The rest had work of political activism experience before entering post-1994 government in both countries.

Another exception of the women I interviewed had begun her political journey in local government. I *was in the local government before, so people who elected me saw me capable of doing... and I had also learnt a lot. So moving from that to the highest place, to the parliament, I had gained a lot of experience (Interview with the author, Kigali, 2013).* However, she had been involved in politics, particularly the RPF liberation movement in exile, before entering government (discussed more below).

Another route to politics for women in politics has been the trade union movement. 18% of women MPs around the world have entered politics having first been involved in trade unions. Leadership in trade unions provides skills and social awareness suitable for politics (Waring et al. 2000). It was in the 1970's in South Africa where women began to be employed in low paying jobs in the manufacturing sector that they started to take on leadership positions in the trade union movement (Graybill 2001). *I started working in a factory at the age of 14, and our first employer was Baas Umtong, [who] was a Chinese. And there were young White girls and White women working there, and young men. But we were treated so badly as Black girls; our lunch hour was 30 minutes and there was a big office dining place but we didn't use that. And everything was just glaringly different for us Blacks and for the Chinese and Whites. And that again made an impact in my head and I began asking questions. So by the time I was 16 in that factory I had managed to organise some of us Black girls to confront Baas Umtong to say, 'this is not on; how can you treat us like this', and of course I was expelled from work (Interview with the author, Pretoria, 2014).* This is the same woman who had been expelled from university for her student activism, as discussed in the chapter on education. This story illustrates that there was not just a class worker/employee divide in the workplace, but also a racial one.

Activism and Armed Struggle

Furthermore, political activism, as seen also in the Education Chapter, became an important aspect of the lives of some of the women I interviewed. A Rwandan woman explained that it was not really a choice, but circumstances that created the impetus for her to become involved in politics. *It was almost like it's not like a choice. You were thrown into it by the fact that you were, you were forced to leave your country by your circumstances. So, the feeling of that injustice, of growing up as a refugee or seeing the conditions your parents were in as refugees, then most definitely when the liberation movement for Rwanda started then it was automatic. When I say we were thrown in to it, it is not with a negative connotation...it is just saying that basically because of the kind of life, the kind of circumstances we were in...So we were not forced. I wasn't forced. I went in very willing, but it's not the same as somebody who grows up in their own country in relative peace and decides that instead of going into research I am going to go into politics. It's not that kind of thing. Because we were doing other things. But at the same time we were in the liberation movement. Our spare time was spent in the liberation movement (Interview with the author, Kigali, 2013).* In other words, activism and politics was done in addition to one's day job, in this instance. Additionally, unlike in some other countries, politics was not a career choice, but something chosen out of conviction created by the circumstances that forced them to leave their home country and live a refugee life.

There were different ways in which the women were political activists. A South African woman played a (but just as crucial) supportive and logistical role in the Anti-Apartheid movement. *In Durban it was particularly difficult; we lived with another girl, we lived in a room which was very hard, we just had a room in Durban; it was really a backyard of an Indian landlord. And these activists at that time they would come and would stay in our room pretending they are visiting us, but instead they are running away from the police. And you know what was also amazing: these men would come and we would sleep all of us in this room, with these men who are hiding, and the next morning they sneak out. And I'm sure the landlady would think that these girls were sleeping with the boys. And sometimes they would leave early. I still remember those things! And it's amazing how those young men – now I talk about them as an old person, I have never seen people who were so disciplined and so respectful; you wouldn't even expect anything like rape or anything like any form of advances. No. No, it was just not done, not known. And sometimes I think the struggle goes, just a kind of a discipline, and everybody can have that discipline. I'm not saying that we were all holy, holy angels; we were not.* Not only did she harbour activists, but she also assisted them in reaching the border to go into exile, *So if I have to do a trip then I have to arrange a workshop or I'm doing an area, and then I will travel and leave the people in the border. I did it year after year because it was the best area. Some people would come from Johannesburg to go to it because I was in this respectable car of the movement.* While she was not an activist herself, she played an important logistical and supporting role that made it possible for

121

activists to evade the Apartheid police and reach exile safely. Women contributed to the struggle in numerous ways, through political and military work, and through emotional and logistical support as well (Graybill 2001). This interviewee, and other South African women I interviewed also had professions outside of politics before 1994, but activism was an important part of their lives. For this interviewee, her work was also tied to some anti-Apartheid activities. *But also I had done a stint for six months in the legal firm, it was for about a year – it was a civil rights law firm which really dealt and represented a lot of young activists in the 1980's...So I think that in a sense also exposed one to some of the political questions and the legal fraternity (Interview with the author, Pretoria, 2014).* The legal profession, and legal literacy, has shown to be an invaluable experience and skill to have, and has served, for some, as an entry into politics (Waring et al. 2000). However, only one of the eleven women that I interviewed was trained as a lawyer, except for the one above who had work experience in a law firm.

An additional route into politics has been that of the armed resistance. Both the RPF and the ANC (while liberation movements) had included women soldiers in their armed wings (Debusscher & Ansoms 2013; Geisler 2000; Herndon & Randell 2013; Powley 2006). A former MK commander explained how she became involved in the armed wing of the ANC. *So I go to Lesotho... then I joined ANC in 1978 and I come in contact with Chris Hani and one comrade who was called Comrade Ace. And at that time when we joined the ANC we were given a choice; 'do you want to go to school or do you want to go to MK?' Most of the time you are persuaded to go to school, especially if you have started with your degree. A group of us, we were about six...so we then say, 'no, we're not going...what we want is to go to the army'. So we get trained underground in Lesotho doing a lot of work with recruitment, recruiting from Lesotho and making contacts. But I finally go for the training in Angola in 1980, but between 1978 and 1980 I was doing the underground work. But whilst you get trained in small firearms you also train others who come from the country...But I finally do my formal military training in 1979 in Angola...then I go to Cuba for further training (Interview with the author, Pretoria, 2014).*

A Rwandan woman that I interviewed was trained in the armed wing of the RPF, but not as a soldier. *But I was not in military. I was a civilian cadre. You know somehow we passed through small training, not as a military career, but we did. There were not a lot of women, but they were there, even women soldiers were there, and civilians too. I think that's how even it came to be that in the government they want to put women in that side (Interview with the author, Kigali, 2013).*

Despite the years of activism and involvement in liberation struggle in South

Africa, some women were not interested in formal politics, but were coerced into it by their comrades and the requirements of the time. *No, how could I have been prepared for it? Firstly, I didn't want to do it; Madiba forced me into it. I had other things I wanted to do in my life (Interview with the author, Johannesburg, 2014).*

Similarly, another South African interviewee wanted to pursue other things. *My activism or my participation in the struggle for liberation wasn't about what am I going to gain afterwards; it was more about what can I do to make sure that we attain our liberation and that we can take the choices that one must take. For instance when I was put on the list in 1994 I refused that because I wanted to go back to school. I had always had a passion of wanting to do my degree but with activism in the 1980s and the spaces where I was it was just not possible. So I said at least 1994 had come, now I can go and study and everybody just said not 'no' (Interview with the author, Pretoria, 2014).*

That some women, after freedom was gained, wanted to leave politics to other people, but were kept by their comrades, speaks to the commitment of the ANC to women's representation, but it also reflect that there was a level of respect and acknowledgement of what women had contributed to the struggle against Apartheid.

The women interviewed here did not enter politics as a career path or choice, as it is viewed in Western countries. It was a combination of the circumstances within which they lived, and a need to change their societies, and reconstruct them. However, the newer generation of politicians in South African enter politics as a career choice. *And people that are getting into politics now are not your original, generationally are not your original revolutionaries. [They] are people that are interested in politics as a career. If you wanted to get into politics you get into the ANC, you pay your R 12 [membership fee], you work, you understand the policy of the ANC and you take that route, you go into parliament. And it does not mean that because you are a young woman, naturally. What we then began not to do as ANC was to train our politicians, all of them, especially women, especially on gender. We don't do that training anymore. We don't do it. And therefore it's not going to be -. And the younger ones are more disadvantaged, both men and women, because they didn't go through my experience (Interview with the author, Pretoria, 2014).*

In essence, this interviewee explains that as opposed to before, when politics was something you are thrown into because of your circumstances (as a Rwandan woman explained earlier), politics in South Africa is now becoming a career choice. Considering the ways in which people were excluded from all kinds of positions of decision-making power before 1994, this is an enormous achievement. However, might be lost in the process is the sense of passion, of sacrifice and working for the greater good that the earlier generation had, that revolutionary spirit to change society.

Conclusion

Around the world there are a myriad of ways in which women enter formal politics and attain positions in government. Many of the Rwandan women interviewed here came from civil society and had been involved in women's organisations or had been doing work involving women's issues. This is a positive thing because it means they were bringing with them not only skills and expertise, but also knowledge of the circumstances of the ordinary women that they worked with.

Entry into politics also appears to be context-specific. Many of these women, both Rwandan and South African, were activists in various ways before 1994. The contexts within which they grew up was a motivating factor. While in western countries the labour force participation of women is an indicator of women's political representation, the same does not hold true in Sub-Saharan Africa. Of the women interviewed here there were two most common paths to formal politics; work experience in civil society, and political activism (including military participation in liberation movements). For many of the South African women who had professional careers outside of politics before 1994, their work still involved them in the social and political issues of the time. In addition, their racial and gender identity restricted them professionally, illustrating the pervasiveness of Apartheid and patriarchy during that time.

However, for both Rwandan and South African women, their ability to receive educations and have jobs/careers placed them at an advantage, as compared to many of their peers, indicating that to some degree they were/are an elite group of women in their respective societies.

Chapter 7: The Three Shifts: Navigating Marriage, Motherhood and Work

'Now how do you translate the policies that you make in your board room into your bedroom?'

Around the world, women face the challenge of balancing their paid work and their work in the home (Seager 2003). Housework is a contested issue within homes, but increasingly within scholarly work as well. In the United States women's labour force participation has increased dramatically, and as a result there has been increasing analysis of the division of labour within the home, as women are traditionally responsible for housework and childcare. Scholars are interested in examining whether women's increased paid work outside the home has affected the gendered division of labour for unpaid housework and childcare. There are findings that women are still overburdened with the bulk of housework. On the other hand, other findings indicate that men are starting to share more responsibilities within the home, and gendered division of labour is decreasing (Bianchi et al. 2000).

The Second Shift

Hochschild & Machung's (1989) seminal work, *The Second Shift: Working Parents and the Revolution at Home*, interrogated the division of labour in the home through empirical data collected over years of interviews with American couples and observing homes. Through this research she coined the term 'Second Shift', which has come to explain the two jobs that most American women have; the first shift is their paid work outside of the home, and the second shift is the unpaid work in the home, such as cooking, cleaning and childcare, which to them feels like being on duty and work. She found that American women shoulder most of the work in the home, creating a gendered leisure gap between men and women.

There are many explanations given for the gendered division of labour within the home. The first explanation is that work hours in the home are determined by who has the most available time for it (because they spend less time performing paid work). The second explanation is that the gendered division of labour is determined by differing power relations between men and women. Who has the power in the home is determined by who brings in the most resources (such as income). Where men make more money, women become dependent on them, and cannot bargain for an equal division of labour. However, a third explanation from feminists is that the gendered division of labour is not determined by time or resource differentials, but by gender relations and performance. In other words, housework and childcare is gendered; being a wife and mother means that you are socially expected to perform the bulk of housework, and one's competence in these roles is determined by standards such as the cleanliness of the home. The gendered performance that is determined by the identities of mother and wife are said to arise from gender socialisation started during childhood, and that people are raised to perform their gender, housework being a form of the woman's performance of her gender.

Studies have shown that when a man and a woman marry, the hours the woman spends on housework increases, whereas the hours the man spends on housework decreases. It has also been shown that even in cases where the husband is economically dependent on his wife, his contribution to housework further decreases as a means of asserting his masculinity. These findings indicate that explanations of time and income differences are not sufficient for explaining the gendered division of labour in the home. Even in more egalitarian homes, women tend to do more housework because they are judged by their homes, whereas men are not. Research has also found that married women (even those who also do paid work) spend more time on housework than unmarried women, whereas men's time spent on housework is not drastically affected by their marital status (Bianchi et al. 2000). While the equal division of childcare and housework is a strategic interest, as opposed to a practical interest (as defined by Molyneux 1985), it is still important, not only for ensuring that women are able to do their best in their political work, but for all women (who want to) to be able to meet their full educational and professional potential.

The unpaid daily work of men and women in the home is not officially considered in the measurements of work. In general, women work longer hours than men, have less leisure time, and perform more tasks than men. Their work in the home is essentially invisible (Seager 2003).

No Equality in the Home

Women MPs around the world have a permanent balancing act of trying to do their work but without it affecting their families, as well as, wrongly or rightly, being criticised for placing their ambitions before the interests of their children. In 1999 60% of 187 women MPs from 65 countries were married. The rest were single, divorced, or widowed. 70% of them had children. 67% of women in the IPU survey expressed the challenge of dividing time between political activities and home life.

In the IPU survey, 80% of respondents received support from partners or husbands, from parents, children or other relatives. 85% of these received support from their husband or partner. Those who received support from husbands or partners said that the household chores had been taken over by them. They also receive help from family members, particularly from their mothers (Waring et al. 2000).

In Rwanda, because of the high male mortality, imprisonment, and emigration, women and children have been left to fend for themselves, meaning that the old ways of doing things have changed (Debusscher & Ansoms 2013). The ratio of men and women was extremely unbalanced after the genocide. It is said that the female population constituted as much as 80% of the entire Rwandan population. As a result, Rwanda has a high proportion of female headed households. In addition, there are decreased opportunities for marriage for women, or to remarry after widowhood or divorce. Gender norms pertaining to the allocation of housework is likely to be changed somewhat due to the changes in the composition of the household, and this is most likely in widow headed households. Those homes that still have the traditional setup of a nuclear family are more likely to abide by old prescribed gender roles. In addition, married women would feel more pressure to abide by these gender roles because of the decreased opportunities for marriage (Schindler 2009).

While women have become active and visible leaders in politics, their roles in the home have not changed as quickly. Even educated and working women face most of the responsibilities of caring for the home and the family. This is a unifying experience amongst women in government, the private sector, and women in the villages (Uwineza & Pearson 2009). A married woman that I spoke to described receiving support from her husband, but he still does not share in the housework and childcare equally. *My husband supports me in all ways he is capable, like during elections he is always there for me, on my side, and sometimes when I have a lot of work and I am not at home he does the dishes, he takes care of the whole family while I am working (Interview with the author, Kigali, 2013)*. However, a further explanation of her husband's support indicates that it is not stable and consistent. *He supports me, but he supports me as a man. A Rwandan man! There are a lot of responsibilities; I come home and I find them waiting for me. For example; cooking. A husband cannot go in the kitchen and cook for you or lay the bed, those are your responsibilities, that's why you find a lot of women have responsibilities. I have to work really hard to do them, that is why I say it is not easy (Interview with the author, Kigali, 2013)*. Her statement of 'a husband', rather than 'my husband', suggests that her husband is performing a socialised gendered division of labour, and not necessarily a personal preference. Her explanation also indicates that this unequal responsibility is tied to the gendered performance of Rwandan men in particular; that they cannot do certain things in the home.

Historically, Rwandan culture glorifies marriage and married people are given respect in society (Uwineza & Pearson 2009). In addition, the status of mothers and motherhood is elevated at all social levels (Herndon & Randell 2013). *In Rwanda, or any other African country, people can't understand when I say I don't have children. But also I found that even in South Africa I remember men telling me, 'you're not an African woman, you're not a true African woman; you're abnormal'. But those are my decisions. But as I say, I had certain moments ...and seeing Hilda's children, there were moments I decided that I'm not going to do [that]. And I don't ever regret decisions about anything. And the only time ever that I thought, 'gosh, I am so lonely' [was] when I was in solitary confinement, that if I had a child outside at least there was something of me (Interview with the author, Kigali, 2013)*. In other words, in both Rwanda and South Africa, women's social status is tied to their motherhood. Lack of children is viewed as unnatural for an African woman. This interviewee, a South African, is one of two who have not had children. All other women I interviewed had at least one child.

Women' Paid Work: Progress or More of the Same?

A question that arose out of my interviews is the degree to which challenges of reconciling paid work and family life are truly centred on motherhood and housework. As I show below, while experiencing the challenge of managing both aspects of their lives, the biggest problem is the attitude of male partners.

My family, me being a single mother, didn't have a problem. But there are some maybe who experience problems... In other words, the difficulties of reconciling political work and family life are exacerbated by male partners, as this woman explained that not having a male partner meant there was no issue in terms of her working outside of the home. Indeed, there seems to be a contradiction in terms of male attitudes and preferences to their wives working outside of the home. On one side they welcome it because it means an added income and improved quality of life for the entire family. However, they do not make much effort to ease the burden on their partners. *As I told you, now every man is aware that a woman also can do it and going there of course is prestigious for your family. It is not for the woman alone. In Rwanda, and maybe Uganda where I was, you'd find the account, the bank account is for the family, not the woman to have her own, that's how I found it. It's not to say that we force it, ok you can have a separate one but later sometimes you find majority of them have one account. So whatever money the woman is going to achieve is for the family, whatever the man is going to achieve it is for the family. So you find they support one another. But where I see maybe they can experience problem maybe after reaching the job, their time, you know, that work is really quite demanding. You work long hours, sometimes even they travel to go abroad. You have younger children, the man is left with the children, or sometimes he also is a politician he has other work. So, it would be there, but not much because I have not heard women complaining about the issue, but it's a problem. So you find you really have a lot, you are stressed out, but you manage it (Interview with the author, Kigali, 2013).* As this interviewee explains, men have come to see the benefits of having a wife who participates in the paid labour force. Today men consider it a sign of development and status to have an educated wife. Working wives also provide another income for the home, which is an incentive for men to support their wives (Uwineza & Pearson 2009). As one woman explained it, men even prefer working women over housewives. *When both men and women [bring an] income at home it will contribute to the development of the family. But if you go and take a woman who can't...generate any income, you will suffer all your life because you are contributing alone to the needs of your family. So I think men of Rwanda...are supportive, because they know what they have ...in terms of efforts in terms of contribution, development (Interview with the author, Kigali, 2013).*

Similarly, before the genocide women were allowed to work or perform other economic activities as long as it did not interfere with their roles as mothers and wives (Herndon & Randell 2013). Despite men's preferences for economically active wives, the allocation of time for housework is characterised along gender lines (Schindler 2009). Essentially, we have to interrogate whether women being allowed to work outside the home, and in this case participate in politics, is an indication of women's social progress and increasing gender equality. Or is it more endemic of women being useful for men's interests, like bringing in an income to ease the economic burden on men? If this is the case, it suggests that women are not necessarily gaining equality in the home, but are having their labour exploited by male spouses for both an extra income and labour in the home.

In Rwandan culture, wives are submissive to their husbands, and even when husbands consult with them, it is the husband who still has the final say on matters. Women's present progress has meant that they are less submissive in this way, which has led to marital problems for some women, though it is not clear how common this is. However, women do feel that it is a positive thing that they are now able to have more of a voice in the home. Women are less likely to stay in unhappy marriages because of their improved rights and economic independence (Burnet 2011). *Because we have this cultural education that consider a man for a place and a woman for another place…so we are fighting this culture in order to educate both girls and boys at the same level, so we think at the end we'll have this understanding of men to do the same work as women, we hope (Interview with the author, Kigali, 2013).*

Despite the progress in terms of women gaining more independence, a voice in the home, and men's willingness for wives to undertake paid work, there are still obstacles to changing cultural prescriptions regarding what women can and can't do. In Rwanda, women heads of households are equated with men and are allowed to take decisions regarding the land and farm. These are widowed or divorced women. However, women still regulate themselves, and it has been found that these women without husbands still refrain from undertaking activities that married women are barred from (such as planting and owning trees for firewood and construction) (Schindler 2009).

Furthermore, ordinary Rwandan women are experiencing a backlash from men in the form of marital discord. Rural women interviewed by Burnet (2011) feel that men are still not recognising their rights. Urban women explained that men feel that women are now acting like men, for example, they have more economic freedom and so they have more personal freedom to do perceived masculine things, such as socialise after work.

Support Structures for the Second Shift

64% of women politicians reported receiving support from their parents, 47% from children, and 40% from other family members. Depending on the cultural context, a large extended family takes over childcare and household work (Waring et al. 2000). The married Rwandan woman, who earlier spoke of her husband not helping with specific tasks, also depends on her extended family for help with childcare. *We have this culture of like being in the family, we have people, we have like cousins, aunties...we live together, we help each other, we love each other, and we have also house helpers. At the end of the day, even if you are tired and you have all that support from your family, a big family, at least you wake up and you're not depressed...So you have something to live for; your family, your kids. You have to work for them and also those people helping you, you have to move on. Our family culture is different from the western countries, so we have some relatives at home and can help so you can perform your [work]. When I am not at home to bring back my kids from school I call my house keeper, tell him 'go with a taxi and pick the kids'. But no, in other countries you must go yourself, you must do all things yourself (Interview with the author, Kigali, 2013).*

72% had the help of domestic workers, who are mostly women. 77.5% of these feel that domestic services are invaluable to them (Waring et al. 2000). Many middle and upper class families in Rwanda have domestic workers to perform the household work (Debusscher & Ansoms, 2013). *But we are still lucky we have helpers, house helpers. So sometimes you can ask him or her for, to do it for you but also she is not there to do everything for you, so you really have to work hard. At the end of the day you are really tired. But all this might end the day men, he can know that we should be equal, to perform equally (Interview with the author, Kigali, 2013).*

For a married South African woman, support came not from her husband, but from her extended family. *So the issues with children and family remain part of your baggage that you need to find a way of managing, I won't say 'balancing'; managing in order to do your work successfully. And for me it was a support system at two levels: one, it was at home, the domestic support system. I was fortunate that my mom was staying with me and my sister was not far away and my brother and my sister who is a nurse by profession. so I knew that when I leave and do my work the kids will not not be attended to. Sometimes they'll tell me when I come back, '[name] was sick, I took him to the doctor' (Interview with the author, Pretoria, 2014).* Essentially, men are not taking equal responsibility for childcare and housework. It falls on the women to depend on an extended support network consisting of relatives and domestic help. Therefore, for these women, equality in politics has not translated into equality in the home.

The gendered division of labour is also the norm in South Africa. During Apartheid women's income was considered secondary to that of her husband, so that it was assumed that even working women were responsible for housework and child care (Hassim 1999).

In exile, the ANC tried to keep families together, but some were separated if parents were deployed. The Women's Section was extremely helpful for mothers, providing a support structure whereby if women were deployed, they could leave their children in the care of crèche's run by the Women's Section. Some women were grateful for this help, while others resented being separated from their children (Hassim 2004).

In MK women were not allowed to have children. In Angola MK women received IUDs (intrauterine devices), which was the policy. Unfortunately, some women became infertile. Those who became pregnant were not allowed to remain in the camps and were taken to Morogoro in Tanzania. For these reasons, women in MK wanted more childcare support from the ANC, so that motherhood would not be an automatic disqualification from active duty. Their argument was that men who impregnated women did not face the same consequences, and were allowed to continue as usual, and even abandon their women and children (Hassim 2004). *And then there's also the question of relations. You are likely to get pregnant and if you get pregnant, wherever you are as a woman, whether MK or not, you get taken to Tanzania where women stay with their children. But the ones that impregnated you don't go; so they continue with their political military careers, so to speak. You can't stay with a child, with a baby, in Angola. But instead of both the men and the women who impregnated each other – no, it's the women who suffer. So biologically, if you have a relationship and condoms were rare at that time, then you are going to be excluded from the mainstream; you do some kind of job in Zambia or in Tanzania. So there's that subtle working of patriarchy where you get excluded by default and the men are left. At some point we did something, in 1981 we did raise this thing that we don't make ourselves pregnant, so why should it be like we are being punished? (Interview with the author, Pretoria, 2014).*

Not only was motherhood regulated in this fashion, but so was marriage. Marriage between ANC women and non-ANC members, such as PAC [Pan Africanist Congress] men, was not allowed and was punished using corporal punishment (which the Women's Section tried, unsuccessfully, to stop). In addition, women were not allowed to marry foreign men as it was believed that women would follow men to their homes, so the ANC would lose if women married foreigners, whereas ANC men were allowed to marry foreign women as this was believed to strengthen the struggle against Apartheid (Hassim 2004). A former MK commander explained that it was difficult for women to date, whereas for men it was easy and beneficial for their quality of life. *And that's the advantage or disadvantage of being a woman in that we had to find bases, bases were people's houses where you can be kept under one guise or another. Now the men found it easier to find girlfriends Batswana girlfriends and then you will stay there and the girlfriend, you can even use the girlfriend for work, even if you find a good girlfriend you can even use that girlfriend to go into the country, do certain things for you. But you were careful; we were getting very little money, we were getting 80 pula per month and that covers your groceries and everything and everything. But if you've got a working girlfriend, she can help. And she cooks for you and then she can invite her own friends and then you can party, in your underground place you can do all these nice things. A woman, where would you find a boyfriend that's going to...cook for you and support you financially and all that? So it's again a question of I talk about – in fact here's a good point – I told about MK in the camp but MK outside when you are operating as a guerrilla outside, you have a disadvantage; the men can mingle nicely and they are not going to be conspicuous. If you are with your girlfriend and nobody's going to be asking you, no, this is a man from South Africa – he's my boyfriend. But I cannot go and approach Tswana men, patriarchy doesn't [allow me to say], 'hey, I love you.' (Interview with the author, Pretoria, 2014).*

After 1994, relationships and marriages remain difficult for South Africa's women leaders. Women politicians interviewed by Britton (2002a) said that their biggest challenge has been personal problems resulting from their workload. Partners and children feel neglected, and there has been a trend of divorces amongst the women. Some of the women moved to Cape Town where the parliament is located, and their husbands did not relocate with them. The physical distance thus puts a strain on relationships. *But also the distance that came with South Africa's political administration where you've got two centres, it does put a strain on the family. And remember I was very young when I got married, I was 30 years in 1995 and he got a job in Johannesburg – so you could see each on the weekend, if you are also not working because I'm most of the time in Cape Town and come in Pretoria once on Thursday night or on Friday and maybe Saturday we have got a deployment in another province where you can't be home (Interview with the author, Pretoria, 2014).*

Indeed, most the first democratic parliamentarians reported struggling to manage their family responsibilities and parliamentary work. Many did not enjoy spending long hours away from their children, even if they were being cared for (Geisler 2000). *...It was very hard in the beginning for women because our parliament was never created in terms of their programmes, to create space for a mother and a wife. And so the early days of transition, having to manage your home; some were very far from Cape Town and you have to fly and then you have to be at home on a Saturday. Oh, what a strain on women, what a strain! When the women get home on a Saturday, each member of parliament who is very busy, she really now has to try and do every possible thing, checking everything in her home. Shopping, everything, you know, name it. And what was the hardest thing is that sometimes it was so difficult for husbands who are not used to managing homes, to really manage a home on their own with the children. At times husbands would phone a wife to say, 'please remind me, I can't remember the name of the doctor of our family. So-and-so is not well, what should I give her?' Yes, little things like that. 'Where do I find the tablets?' Little things that seem little which are taken for granted that any mother will do, and of course men, not that they don't want to, they have never had an opportunity to get to know about school uniforms and the crisis of homework: that was the greatest thing because in situations where people still had smaller kids...But to be away from home was really quite a challenge in the early days, and of course like everything else it took its own adjustment.*

In addition, husbands were not able to cope with their wives' workload, becoming suspicious of affairs, and others just did not like having wives with a higher status than them (Geisler 2000). *Because in a sense it doesn't matter whether you might have been activists together, which we are and have always been, but there's the reality that comes with the responsibility of power. And sometimes men, because they've never been accustomed to not be in front and to be the ones that are recognised and you are always recognised with reference to him. It becomes a kind of difficulty where for the first time it will be like, 'this is [her] husband, as opposed to [his] wife'. That you could tell was a bit of a struggle (Interview with the author, Pretoria, 2014).*

All of these challenges and pressures, largely created by a patriarchal society wherein it is not the norm for women to commute for work, and it is not the norm for men to have the bulk of childcare and housework, meant that many marriages failed. Many women MPs divorced, with as much as 30 in the first year alone (Geisler 2000). *Yes, I was married like many people were married; but the other big thing about politics is you don't actually have a life. You don't have a life, your life doesn't belong to you. It's difficult: if I think of everyone that I know, there's one couple that's still married, otherwise every single person that I know is divorced (Interview with the author, Kigali, 2013).*

However, some of the divorces might also be a sign that women were feeling empowered to leave oppressive marriages (Geisler 2000). In addition, as one woman explained, while not everyone in South African politics has headed for divorce, there are those who are living dysfunctional marriages. *But what may be silent and not said is how many families got [broken], people might not have come out of their marriages but a serious impact were there were children out of wedlock. Some of those things that people wouldn't talk about, you'd want to create a brave face and say, 'ja, everything was just fine'.*

Similarly to the pressures that exist in Rwanda regarding marital relationships, South African women are often blamed for their husband's infidelities, particularly if she is a busy working woman. *And unfortunately our society...will justify it, 'what are they going to do bantu?' You know, it's like, 'if your physical presence is not there, what do you expect this man to do?' But if a man would be going to work in the mines for nine months, the woman must be faithful and stay. So I'm saying you might have a definite number for people who have divorced but you might have an equal number of those who have stayed but in collapsed relationships where either it's a fear of reprisal amongst the community or maybe...what is on your psyche, liberated as you might be, but there's that thing...(Interview with the author, Pretoria, 2014).* What suggests that it is patriarchal socialisation, more than anything else, which has caused the breakdown of marriages, is the fact that it has disproportionately been the case for women MPs, and not men MPs. Furthermore, it is the social pressures, as indicated above, which force some women to remain in unhappy marriages.

In addition, women may not make the sacrifice to stay in unhappy marriages because of social pressures, but also because of feelings of responsibility and guilt to maintain a family unit for the children. *Secondly, it's like you've brought shame into your family that you couldn't hold it together....But I personally have experienced it that when time comes you then make the call, not for you more than anything; you ask yourself, 'if I go at this moment what is the impact on the children? Will they cope or will it destroy them?' And unfortunately nobody does a research to test how these children will behave. You make an assumption and make yourself a sacrificial lamb and say it may not be hunky-dory anymore but maybe just for the stability of these children for now until they are old enough maybe I need to stay. So I'm saying you have a lot of those where certain considerations had to be made to just say these twins – and particularly when you've got boy kids – I mean, you would see boy children who are born and stayed with single mothers at some stages like they go berserk...But it's an issue of identity because culturally your identity, particularly the man is defined through his father; not that people don't value the work that your mom might have done in raising you up but there's this expectation in our society still that you need a father figure, just like the mother figure gives them. But a father figure you need – so part of those struggles of decision making for women to take a choice that will be better for them is again governed by these cultural norms and dynamics.*

The cultural factors seem enormous; one woman interviewed by Britton (2002a) felt that women have two choices; they can either be wives and be married, or they can be autonomous, independent and fulfilled women. In other words, there is a sense that it is not possible to have both.

Considering that these were women who passed important legislation that empowered women in customary marriages, gave them access to abortion on demand, and passed legislation giving women child support from the fathers of their children, those who chose to remain in unhappy marriages present a contradictory story. *Well, if one were to take this issue we are talking about now, if you look at the calibre of all of us who went to parliament you can't say it's women who didn't participate in the women's struggle, it's women who didn't know what you had to do, women who didn't know their rights, it's women who didn't know there are choices, that how many choices are there that you can make; it's women who have drafted the very laws. But when a woman is faced with those choices, knowing all of those things there are other considerations that a person takes a choice around to say: do I, do I not? (Interview with the author, Pretoria, 2014).* In other words, creating policy and legislation is one thing, but having to live with the social and personal consequences of being an empowered woman is a challenge and burden of its own.

Managing Childcare

All of this indicates the tough choices that women face, and that being married can actually be a disability in terms of quality of life, productivity and happiness. Managing marriages appears to be the biggest personal challenge faced by women. While childcare is also difficult, those who have children manage to find ways to make that aspect work. Balancing these various roles requires careful planning and time management (Waring et al. 2000). *So as a woman, as a mother, if it happens to you don't say, 'I am tired, I don't have time'. You must organise yourself to have time for your family. And if sometimes when I have a few minutes, I am going to prepare for you, whatever I prepare, even if I make bananas...I used to make such surprise, to show them I am care, I take care of*

136

them (Interview with the author, Kigali, 2013).

In addition, in most parliaments around the world the institution has not been transformed to accommodate the family commitments of women MPs (Waring et al. 2000). In South Africa there is the availability of a crèche within the parliament, but this is not the norm, and is not available in Rwanda either (Waring et al., 2000). Unlike in South Africa where the parliament's working hours and calendar have been changed to accommodate women's home life, this also has not happened in Rwanda (Devlin & Elgie 2008). An MP interviewed by Devlin & Elgie (2008) said that parliament operates as normal regardless if there are more women. They found that women MPs did not make a connection between their parliamentary work and their domestic responsibilities. They argue that balancing home life and work is a challenge that all women face, and is not unique to them, and therefore parliament is not obligated to make adjustments just for them. Rather, their balancing act takes place within the home, and solutions are found there.

However, no matter who takes over the responsibilities in the home and childcare, women often try to compensate for their absence by being emotionally and mentally present for their children when they are home, such as helping with homework, paying special attention to them, etc. Interestingly, women from developing countries pay particular attention to their children's school needs, such as organising professional educational support such as governess', boarding schools, etc. (Waring et al. 2000). *And actually I decided to pay for my daughter to be in day boarding, to avoid her to be alone at home because she is not in a boarding school, but I am lucky the school developed a kind of day boarding...after school they do extra curricula activities and they go back to the classrooms, helped by teachers to do their homework, then they go home to sleep every day. I decided to take the program to avoid her being at home alone. And when I finish my work late we meet always at home.*

The end of the sexual division of labour and the sharing of childcare and domestic work between the sexes would be strategic interests, as defined by Molyneux (1985). However, I would argue that that these are also practical gender interests, particularly in the context of developing countries such as Rwanda and South Africa. Where women are over-burdened with household work, they have less time to spend on their educations and income-generating activities, thereby entrenching women's disproportionate levels of poverty. It is a blurry line and perhaps falls between the categories of strategic and practical gender issues.

'Are men asked these questions?! I try to be present at the weekend. It is a choice that does not always go down well outside the family – too bad. I am often

busy with meetings. Some think that I should put looking after the home above everything else: after all I am only a woman' (as quoted in Waring et al. 2000: 151).

This is an important point; that the question itself is sexist and is based on the underlying assumptions that women perform caretaking roles in the home. It does not include the assumption that not all women are mothers or wives. In addition, it makes the assumption that home life and professional life cannot be complementary, but are always in conflict. Men are not asked and surveyed about how they balance their home life with their political careers; it is assumed that they have a woman who is taking care of the home while they are out pursuing their careers in politics. The above quote also indicates that at times the tension is not even in the home, it is from society and their expectations of what roles should take precedence in a woman's life. For example, some of the women I interviewed expressed the pride that their children have in them because of the work that they do. *They are fans. For my children I am not a leader, actually I am not a leader, I am a woman. Proud to be a woman, and proud to play my role. Sometimes I tell my children 'whatever I'll be called to do, even cleaning, if I feel my role today is to clean this room I will clean it. At home I am a mother, I am a woman, and I am a friend of my family (Interview with the author, Kigali, 2013).*

Another woman expressed the particular pride her work as a woman parliamentarian has instilled in her daughter, and that she has become a role-model for her. *She likes it. She's proud of it. And sometimes she will say, 'mummy, I am growing up, I will replace you when you have gone'. That's what she used to tell me, and even up to today she is a lawyer, she is an international lawyer. She is a lawyer, so she says, 'ah, one time I will be in your seat there'. So I think she likes it. She likes the job because its maybe it never stressed me up, she could see I was comfortable and elected, so she says one time I will replace you there (Interview with the author, Kigali, 2013).*

Some women politicians have made the choice not to have children specifically because of the demanding nature of politics (Waring et al. 2000). ... *I had a woman who was doing translation for me, because my Xhosa is not that good. That was in Gugulethu and every Saturday I'd go to Crossroads and I'd pick her up at her house; and in Gugulethu they had these back, she had a Wendy house, and she came out all very smartly dressed...and there were her sick children, all little children, crying, dirty and wanting her attention. And I said, 'It's okay, you don't have to go with me, I can go on my own.' And, 'No, no, no, no, I'll go with you.' And that was the moment where I decided; how do you actually work for a greater cause to have a better society and a new society with women's liberation and equality and no apartheid and you don't actually feed your children? And that was the moment that I decided that I was not going to have children (Interview with the author, Kigali, 2013).*

The above story indicates the determination and passion that was felt for South Africa's liberation; and the sacrifices that went into ensuring that that vision was attained. Yet, on the other end of the spectrum, many women are hesitant to run for parliament because of their personal responsibilities, including the social identification of women as mothers (Waring et al. 2000). Indeed, childcare has been identified as one of the major barriers to women's political participation (Goetz et al 2009). That there are two such extremes in some of the choices that some women make; either having children and foregoing politics or not having children at all, indicates that the gendered division is not only a social construction that needs to be abolished for the sake of making women's lives easier. It is also important to address it because it is one of the ways that gender inequality is entrenched and maintained. Prominent ANC MP, the Late Ruth Mompati said, 'Even the establishment of our crèche is a reminder to the Government that unless the sexual division of labour is challenged, and unless men take equal responsibility for parenting, women will remain unequal,' (cited in Britton 2002a: 56).

For one woman who had a child while an activist. *But there are also things that in the political sphere, you've got to compromise. There's got to be knowledge that at some point you can then say, 'no, I can't do this, my children'. I have a son who's emotionally [cold] because I've never mothered him, and now I feel so bad because I've created the conditions now. But what I've lost – because I was never there, even when I was there I was not there. So now with my son there's a cold character, you can say to him… '…I've bought you an aeroplane that you wanted.' He'll say, 'Just park it there, I'm still watching TV.' 'Okay, where is that aeroplane? Oh, it's beautiful.' He's just like that (Interview with the author, Pretoria, 2014).*

In particular, she cautions against glorifying the personal sacrifices of women activists, and to not view their subsequent political prominence as a happily-ever-after story of women's empowerment and liberation. *And that's the part that I find with the younger generation is not there – it's either people are completely radical or completely subservient and they use us older women as examples that we have made it and you made it on your own and there's Brigalia Bam, there's Frene Ginwala…But they don't know that in fact we sacrificed that part and sometimes unnecessarily, we could have balanced. When my partner died, I could sit down and say, ja, for men I could have balanced, I could have met him half-way without going down the road, just negotiate with him. I could even have ne-*

gotiated that, okay, let's take two years off and go to Tanzania, you do something and I'll do something and we have this baby and we take it from there. But I just said no. And when we came back there was no need for me to then say that I couldn't be in negotiation if I'm pregnant; I could have been. But it was going to be this focus that I just said no. So it's something that people have got to really balance because you only have one life and it cannot be just a political life as I think I had, mine was just a political life and nothing else. Fun – you've got to have fun within that political life! We've got to live, you live only once (Interview with the author, Pretoria, 2014).

Steps to Achieving Equality in the Home

She went on to explain that achieving a balance means steady but gradual changes within the private sphere, in personal relationships. *And you should be aware that it's not yet time. For instance, you've got to even go to be a little bit backward and it's very amazing coming from me that if in the house you usually cook and share responsibility, when there are the in-laws then you must, because you don't want your husband to be viewed as a sissy or whatever. You introduce this a little bit by your husband one time bringing tea to his mother but you don't just start, 'Please can you make tea for us there?' and then sit down to chat to your mother-in-law or your relatives (Interview with the author, Pretoria, 2014).*

Amongst South African women especially, I sensed not regret, but a feeling of sadness of having missed out on having normal relationships, of missing out on motherhood (whether not having children or not being present mothers) and having a normal family life. *I have moved on; I actually have to do things for myself now, I must stop having to struggle and be the martyr – you don't have a life, you don't have a marriage, you don't have a relationship, you don't have anything, because everything actually was a struggle. And I think if you'd ask me if I'd do it again I'd say yes because I believe in what I do. But I also think that we must get some more humanity into our struggle...but I need to sleep, I need to eat, I need to exercise, I need to look after my family, I need to have a social life, I must have a balanced life – it's nothing about that (Interview with the author, Kigali, 2013).* This, and the next story, illustrate the complete dedication that some activists had for the elimination of Apartheid and the creation of a democratic and equal society. *And I was one-track minded, I must confess. It's one of those times that -. Sometimes I think I could have done things differently, but being a woman I just was very, very passionate about overthrowing apartheid. There was nothing that occupied me or my mind. My late partner was also somewhat – but I didn't form relationships, I didn't do anything except -. I guess leadership may have recognised that this one-track mindedness. And I hated apartheid with every fibre of my body and I was quite clear that we can and we have to do something about it (Interview with the author, Pretoria, 2014).*

Despite the loss of certain aspects of a fulfilling life, these stories help us to understand the very real human costs of Apartheid outside of the more visible inequalities and human rights crimes. Even those who survived the Apartheid state as activists, and played a pivotal role in South Africa's transition and early democracy, there is a sacrifice that cannot be compensated.

As the stories from Rwanda and South Africa have shown, there is the argument that norms do not change quickly, despite the influence of major events (Schindler 2009). Women in politics face some of the same personal battles that other working women face. They face the challenge of trying to balance their work life with their roles as partners, mothers, and daughters (Waring et al. 2000). Some feminists have argued that unpaid work should be considered in social policy, but that raises the question of how do we acknowledge women's work in the home without continually essentialising this gendered division of labour? (Hassim 1999).

The Third Shift

A recent body of work looking at women's paid and unpaid is starting to show that many women also experience a third shift. That is; they have their paid work outside of the home, their unpaid work within the home, as well as other activities that require their time and attention (which is largely also unpaid). For example, third shift literature has explained that women who do care work are performing a third shift. Such work includes taking care of elderly parents, taking care of friends in difficult circumstances, or volunteering in social activities such as soup kitchens or church activities.

Women may also work in family-owned businesses without financial compensation, and their labour therein is largely invisible. The third shift also includes women who further their education while working and being wives and mothers. Another example of the third shift that women experience are farm wives. Women who have paid work outside of the farm are found, in the United

States, to participate in farm work as regularly as unemployed women on farms (Gallagher & Delworth 1993; Gerstel 2000; Kramarae 2000; Lee et al. 2006).

Another factor affecting marriages, as has been found in Rwanda, particularly for women in governance, are the responsibilities in the home and in the community. Husbands with wives in local governance feel that their own homes are not benefitting from their wives' positions. Local level officials do not receive salaries for their work, but still spend a significant amount of time fulfilling their responsibilities and participating in community meetings, labour and trainings. This leaves rural women especially with less time to work in the fields and no financial compensation. Husbands then become resentful of this. Unfortunately for many of these women, they cannot afford to hire extra labour to help them with their work in the home and the fields (Burnet 2011).

In Rwanda, women work second and third shifts (Herndon & Randell 2013). In addition, women have the double-burden of trying to include gender perspectives into a range of issues, such as foreign affairs, as well as their official duties (Powley 2005). Essentially, they perform the same work as their male colleagues, but have the added responsibility of representing women's interests in everything that they do (Powley 2006; Uwineza & Pearson 2009). One woman interviewed by Uwineza & Pearson (2009) said that women feel more comfortable approaching women leaders than male leaders. As a result, women will bring their grievances to women leaders, even those who do not hold official women's or gender posts. The women leaders then have to refer and explain the issue to the men who are working in the relevant office or department.

In other cases, women voluntarily take on other work that is not in their job descriptions. *There is an association to help women, like widows, like building houses for them, for poor people. Like you know we have a lot of orphans in Rwanda due to the Rwandan genocide, we build houses for them. We did stuff like that. It was our extra mandate because our mandate is to make laws and the control over the government. So, we had other extra activities. Women in the parliament (Interview with the author, Kigali, 2013).* Other extra activities that Rwanda's women MPs participate in include, *Programs, workshops, because when we were in the parliament we don't sit there and keep quiet, especially as I said, in each province at least you get 6 women representatives there in parliament, so then we say we have to go back, work with them, organise training, sometimes with civil society they can help us especially with the funds...when you work with the civil society organisations that are there they can organise and you go and you do lessons...(Interview with the author, Kigali, 2013).*

South African women MPs also face a double workload. They have their committee work, and they also participate in gender committees, or women's groups, or their party's women's caucuses. As a result, they are disproportionately burdened with representing women and gender issues, thereby doing more work than men (Britton 2002a). For example, their third shift work is also of a social care nature, like the Rwanda MPs. One woman described being involved in a small volunteer program with her church members. *One of our women doctors has a list of all the patients, her patients who are very sick, very poor, and she knows that. They come to the surgery and she will do home visits; and she asked us if we will adopt the family. We don't know them – and every month we do grocery for them. Not one person in the church who won't do that. Not one. And then we are given a list and then you look at the list and you think this list, no, that's too small. And nobody is going to say, 'oh, if I buy this grocery once a month I'm going to be poor', I can assure you. (Interview with the author, Pretoria, 2014).*

This and other such cases show that 'representation' is not always institutionalised, structural, or legislative. Speaking of a South African system where qualifying people can collect a monthly grant to assist with supporting children in the home. *You know, one male ambassador, we were talking about health and we had a presentation from the minister of health and he was talking about this question of pregnancy grants and he was saying that there's no evidence that in fact people get pregnant because they want this money. So there were men that were arguing that they [women] want [a] child to get the grant. But one man...was making an example that, 'there's this woman who keeps on getting pregnant and it's because of this money'. And he was saying, 'why don't [we] have a way of just sewing them up so that they don't keep on just processing these children'. Sewing them! So, of course, as women we said he has to withdraw, and he couldn't find a reason why he should withdraw. And we were saying what about sewing the man because they produce the sperm; why don't you sew the men instead of sewing the women? (Interview with the author, Pretoria, 2014).* In other words, the meeting changed from discussing this particular welfare program, to a scenario where women had to fight against the sexist attitude of a colleague. However, the greater implication of this story is that individuals with sexist attitudes, such as this, have decision-making power over women's every-day lives and survival. Rather than discussing the true pros and cons of the program, women in the meeting had to battle sexism and mysoginy by their colleague.

Again, another example shows that the third shift may constitute helping to conscietise male colleagues on women's and gender issues, instead of focusing on the task at hand. *I mean just if I was to share with you one anecdote, in Cabinet, once one minister brings in a memo for an advisory committee; I think one woman out of 10 – and instinctively all of us as women just said no, and his answer was 'Well, I don't know women in this sector.' So I said, 'You don't know them, we'll find them for you.' The president said, 'yes'. We did suspend that memo that day, it didn't pass. We looked for women, and said, 'here they are, here's their profiles'. And we had to insist that there must be a database because if men ministers say they don't know women, so let's have a database with all women so that you can't argue and say you don't know women (Interview with the author, Pretoria, 2014.* In trying to both conscietise men, and ensure that women are equally included, the women MPs had to become recruitment agents, taking them away from their mandate and official job descriptions, which of course could not go undone either.

In other instances, the third shift is not about serving or helping others, but there is the extra pressure of having to prove themselves, simply because they are women. *They've got to be vigilant because if you make blunders as a woman, it's not taken as, 'this minister has blundered', it's 'this woman!'. And therefore, because society doesn't expect much of us, just like the white people didn't expect much of a black government, so we've got to be vigilant that we don't fall into that trap of really proving that. So as a woman you've got to do that (Interview with the author, Pretoria, 2014).* For one woman this meant working extra hours. *So you had to drive yourself and work more; you had to work extra hours to try and make sure that there are no mistakes, because if there are it's not going to be about X has – it will be, 'you see? Women!'* (Interview with the author, Pretoria, 2014).

This pressure to prove themselves as competent to be in politics and government began before the ANC came to power, including in the military camps. *You've got to prove yourself on the terrain in everything that you do – because there's this thing that you cannot make it, you are a woman. If you really want to be taken seriously you've got to do more than what the men do; you've got to exercise more than they do. You've got to practice more than they do. You've got to just make sure that you are ahead of the men. But that makes your own consciousness as a woman that here I've got to outdo...even in the camps I personally decided that there's not a single thing that I'm not going to be good at. And I suffered from arthritis, my left knee. But it didn't matter how painful it was, I was not going to say I can't do this thing because of my health problem. When we went to the USSR it was snowing, it was mid-winter and I was the only woman in a group of eight. And there was something that I couldn't quite do well, it was sliding across, holding onto something, they put a wire this side and a wire – and then you cross a river. I couldn't do that, I couldn't hold. And each time you fall you are going to fall and hit a dam, a small dam, you're going to hit the dam with your body. And of course the dam is frozen and you're going to walk back again to where you started and do it again until you do it. You don't have gloves, you are holding onto this Slippery rod and it's slippery because of ice. And you've got to move very fast...And I told myself this thing, there is no way that I'm going to be exempted. So I would creep out at night and agree with the guard that I am going there so that I can do this thing and practice and practice and practice and practice and practice and practice until I master it (Interview with the author, Pretoria, 2015).* The pressure to prove themselves is not abnormal or excessive in the circumstances. Women's roles in politics and as leaders are still under scrutiny, so they are harder on themselves than even men are (Herndon & Randell, 2013).

When asked about women's leadership in Rwanda, one interviewee expressed that there is this general sense amongst women leaders (though not all) that they have to make sure that they are capable and competent exactly because they are being scrutinised. Perhaps the pressure is doubly-so because they are being scrutinised by virtue of their gender, in ways that men are not. *They are individuals. You have good leaders, you have those who are not such good leaders. I tend, I try not to go into the sentimental arguments about how women are nurturers, you know, so they'll be tender, they understand people more than that. But I think maybe because of the fact that women haven't been in very obvious positions of leadership before, when they get into leadership positions, they have at the back of their minds they have to prove themselves. Nobody is watching a man to see how they perform. But women, they know definitely that they have to prove themselves, so in many ways that means that they make an extra effort (Interview with the author, Kigali, 2013).*

Conclusion

I think that patriarchy is a deep, deep, deep ingrained thing and it's not going to change overnight. And I think the reason why gender equality and sexism is such a critical thing [is] because it actually means you've got to change inside. And I joke about it, when I was a gender commissioner I would go to these ministries and I'd challenge the ministries and I'd say: Now how do you translate the policies that you make in your board room into your bedroom – because that's where the crux of gender equality is – you know, the sexual relationships, the power at that intimate relations, you know (Interview with the author, Kigali, 2013).

Patriarchy and the gendered division of labour is a common experience for Rwandan and South African women interviewed here. While most women have found ways to manage their roles as mothers and leaders, marriages have been the biggest personal challenge for women who hold political leadership positions. Those who are married do not share the load with their husbands, but with a support network of extended family and friends. For some women the personal life has been an area of sacrifice for a greater cause, such as foregoing childcare or motherhood altogether.

Another common experience that has emerged from these stories is that women not only experience the first shift (their paid work), the second shift (unpaid work in the home) but they also experience a variety of third shifts. These range from social service work, to being vigilant of sexism amongst their colleagues, or even working harder and longer hours than men because they are aware that they are being more closely scrutinised.

In summation, if we are to explore women political leaders, it is helpful to understand their challenges, as well as to contextualise them. Particularly by understanding their personal lives, we find a space in which they are generally connected to most other women's experiences, who also face conflicts trying to manage all their roles. All of this is to say that patriarchy does not discriminate. Even for those women to ascend to positions of power, patriarchy continues to dominate their lives in visible and invisible ways.

Conclusion

Much has been written and discussed on women in politics in Rwanda and South Africa. Both countries, particularly their ruling parties, have shown a commitment to achieving gender equality in political representation. However, the nature and quality of that representation has come in to question. On Rwanda, the main question has been whether women's leadership is legitimate, or whether it is a means of furthering a particular political agenda. Similarly in South Africa, the level of women politician's representation of women's interests has been interrogated.

It is difficult to determine what women's interests are, and sometimes various stakeholders have different interpretations. Rwandan and South African women politicians have seemed to focus on practical gender interests, those issues that affect women immediately; issues of survival. For example, Rwanda has passed the Inheritance Law which has significantly improved women's legal status in Rwandan society. It gives them rights to, amongst other things, inherit property and receive credit without a husband's permission. South Africa has passed the customary marriages act, which also significantly improves women's rights in terms of protecting them in the cases of traditional marriages. For example, they have gained equal rights to their children. Also, institutions have been created and transformed to include and address gender equality and women's interests, respectively. Similarly, in both countries, perceptions regarding political leadership as a masculine domain are changing. However, in South Africa the change appears to be much slower as women politicians are routinely attacked on the basis of their gender by the public and politicians alike.

Therefore, the argument that women's representation in Rwanda and South Africa has been ineffectual diminishes the monumental achievements for women, and the steps that have been made towards achieving gender equality in the societies. This is not to say that gender equality has been attained, nor that the standard of living for the majority of women in these countries has been drastically improved.

Rather, a more nuanced understanding is necessary to understand the successes, and what challenges remain. In this regard, perhaps what stands out in the discourse on this topic is the manner in which the burden of representing women's interests is overwhelmingly placed on the shoulders of women politicians, regardless of whether they are quota representatives or not. Perhaps exploring these issues, from their perspectives, can help to illuminate where the disconnect lies between what they believe they ought to be doing, and what outsiders want to see happen. An outsider here refers to different interest groups such as women, children, men academics, activists, researchers, etc. (although of course even within these groups there is diversity in needs and interests).

To understand the issues pertaining women in politics I interviewed eleven women; six in Rwanda and five in South Africa. I found that they are an advantaged group of women. All of them have received formal educations, though most of them did so in the most trying circumstances. Their achievement in this regard speaks to their characters as individuals, as well as the people who supported and sacrificed for them, such as parents. Those that worked before taking up political leadership did paid work in the formal sector, again an advantaged experience compared to many women in their countries. However, political and social activism has been a major part of most of their lives. For many, their consciousness arose out of experiences during their childhoods and early adult life. I suggest that those experiences continue to influence them today in terms of their political priorities. In the case of Rwanda the need is to create a stable society and growing economy to root out the causes of the historical strife. In South Africa the priority is to address all forms of inequality, not only those pertaining to gender. Furthermore, it is incorrect to examine the impact of women's representation without considering the various identities that they might ascribe to, and the political priorities that arise from these. For example, in Rwanda, social unity is as much a priority as gender equality. Similarly, in South Africa racial all equality is as much a priority as gender equality.

In addition, in some instances, such early experiences and activism forced them to make sacrifices within their personal lives. Motherhood, particularly, is an area in which great sacrifices have been made where mothers have not been able to be present for their children, or have had to sacrifice motherhood altogether (where they may have chosen to become mothers in different circumstances).

Even after the advent of peace and the attainment of formal political leadership, their personal lives continue to be areas of difficulty. Marriages suffer, and managing their professional lives and childcare has been a challenge. Significantly, while they have progressed in achieving more equality for women in politics, the home has been an area where progress has been slower. Based on this, it is false to assume that this particular group of women has no connection to the experiences of ordinary women. This is especially the case seeing, as I argue, that the inequality that they experience within the home is a result of continued patriarchal attitudes regarding the roles of women and men. The contradiction between this public progress and private stagnation suggests that changing personal attitudes and lifestyles is much harder than changing policy.

From this arises two questions; firstly, what are the challenges that women politicians face, and secondly, how can we hold government and all politicians accountable for representing women's interests? Perhaps the first step is to place less emphasis on looking at women as a collective to be held accountable, but by exploring the work of particular individuals. A follow-up would be to determine where accountability is failing in terms of whether women in general consider gender equality an important policy in their voting preferences. I suggest that it is important to move away from the view that there is no accountability because of the electoral system which makes officials accountable to the parties and not constituents. It has been shown that political parties will select women candidates and include women's interests in their policy if they believe that they would win more votes from women. Therefore, the drive should come from ordinary women to hold the parties accountable. As I have tried to show, women politicians in Rwanda and South Africa have achieved a great deal in terms of advancing the interests of women. Where failures have happened, they have been the result of a lack of social and political will. For example, the business sector's opposition to the gender equality bill of South Africa, and the lack of funding for NGM in both countries, respectively.

Therefore, the impact of the increased representation of women in Rwanda and South Africa's national politics should no longer be examined in terms of what the women have achieved, but rather, what has the society achieved and what still needs to be done.

Bibliography

Adler, N.J., 1996. Global Women Political Leaders: An Invisible History, an Increasingly Important Future. *Leadership Quarterly*, 7(1), pp. 133–161.

Ballington, J., 1998. Women's Parliamentary Representation: the Effect of List PR. *Politikon: South African Journal of Political Studies*, 25(2), pp. 77-93.

Barnes, T.D. & Burchard, S.M., 2013. "Engendering" Politics: The Impact of Descriptive Representation on Women's Political Engagement in Sub-Saharan Africa. *Comparative Political Studies*, 46(7), pp. 767–790.

Bauer, G., & Britton, H.E., 2006. *Women in African Parliaments*. Boulder: Lynne Rienner Publishers.

Bauer, G., 2011. Sub-Saharan Africa. In: Bauer, G. & Tremblay, M. (Eds.) *Women in Executive Power: A Global Overview*, 1st ed. London: Routledge., pp. 85-99.

Bianchi, S.M, Milkie, M.A., Sayer, L.C. & Robinson, J.P., 2000. Is Anyone Doing the Housework? Trends in the Gender Division of Household Labor. *Social Forces*, 79(1), pp. 191-228.

Bratton, K.A., 2005. Critical Mass Theory Revisited: The Behaviour and Success of Token Women in State Legislatures, *Politics and Gender*, 1(1), pp. 97-125.

Britton, H.E., 2002. Coalition Building, Election Rules, and Party Politics: South African Women's Path to Parliament, *Africa Today*, 49(4), pp. 33-67.

b. Britton, H., 2002. The Incomplete Revolution, *International Feminist Journal of Politics*, 4(1), pp. 43-71.

Britton, H.E., 2008. Challenging Traditional Thinking on Electoral Systems. In: Tremblay, M. (ed.). *Women and Legislative Representation*, 1st ed. New York: Palgrave Macmillan., pp. 117-128.

Budlender, D., 2000. Introduction. The Fifth Women's Budget. Internationalbudget.org [Online]. Available at http://internationalbudget.org/wp-content/uploads/Introduction-to-the-Fifth-Womens-Budget-Initiative.pdf [Accessed 5 May 2015].

Burnet, J.E., 2008. Gender Balance and the Meanings of Women in Governance in Post-Genocide Rwanda. *African Affairs*, 107(428), pp. 361–386.

Burnet, J.E., 2011. Women have Found Respect: Gender Quotas, Symbolic Representation, and Female Empowerment in Rwanda. *Politics & Gender*, 7, pp. 303-334.

Celis, K., Childs, S., Kantola, J. & Krook, M.L., 2008. Rethinking Women's Substantive Representation. *Representation*, 44(2), pp. 99–110.

Childs, S. & Krook, M.L., 2009. Analysing Women's Substantive Representation: From Critical Mass to Critical Actors. *Government and Opposition*, 44(02), pp. 125–145.

Coffe, H., 2012. Conceptions of Female Political Representation. Perspectives of Rwandan Female Representatives, *Women's Studies International Forum*, 35, pp. 286-297.

Curnow, R., 2000. Thandi Modise, A Woman in War. *Agenda: Empowering Women for Gender Equity*, 16(43), pp. 36-40.

Dagne, T., 2011. *Rwanda□: Background and Current Developments.* Library of Congress Washington DC Congressional Research Service [online]. Available at: www.crs.gov [Accessed 5 May 2015].

Dahlberg, L. & McCaig, C., 2010. Practical Research and Evaluation: A Start-to-Finish Guide for Practitioners. London: Sage Publications.

Dahlerup, D. & Freidenvall, L., 2005. Quotas as A "Fast Track" to Equal Representation for Women. *International Feminist Journal of Politics*, 7(1), pp. 26–48.

Dahlerup, D., 2007. Electoral Gender Quotas: Between Equality of Opportunity and Equality of Result. *Representation*, 43(2), pp. 73–92.

Dahlerup, D., 2006. The Story of the Theory of Critical Mass. *Politics & Gender*, 2(04), pp. 491–530.

Davis, R., 2015. Analysis: The Dress that Brought the Mpumalanga Legislature to a Standstill. *Daily Maverick*, [online]. Available at: http://www.dailymaverick.co.za/article/2015-04-01-analysis-the-dress-that-brought-the-mpumalanga-legislature-to-a-standstill/#.VUeGw_mqqkp [Accessed 4 May 2015].

Debusscher, P. & Ansoms, A., 2013. Gender Equality Policies in Rwanda: Public Relations or Real Transformations? *Development and Change*, 44(5), pp. 1111-1134.

Devlin, C. & Elgie, R., 2008. The Effect of Increased Women's Representation in Parliament: The Case of Rwanda. *Parliamentary Affairs*, 61(2), pp. 237–254.

Eagly, A.H., 2007. Female Leadership Advantage and Disadvantage: Resolving the Contradictions. *Psychology of Women Quarterly*, 31(1), pp. 1–12.

Eagly, A.H. & Johannesen-Schmidt, M.C., 2001. The Leadership Styles of Women and Men. *Journal of Social Issues*, 57(4), pp. 781–797.

Eagly, A.H., Johannesen-Schmidt, M.C. & van Engen, M.L., 2003. Transformational, transactional, and laissez-faire leadership styles: a meta-analysis comparing women and men. *Psychological Bulletin*, 129(4), pp. 569–591.

Eagly, A.H. & Johnson, B.T., 1990. Gender and leadership style: A meta-analysis. *Psychological Bulletin*, 108(2), pp. 233–256.

Electoral Commission of South Africa, 2015. Candidate Lists [online]. Available at: http://www.elections.org.za/content/Elections/Candidates-lists/ [Accessed 26 February 2015].

Ensor, L., 2014. Gender Bill Cracks National Assembly Nod Despite Quorum Woes. *Business Day Live* [online]. Available at: http://www.bdlive.co.za/business/2014/03/05/gender-bill-cracks-national-assembly-nod-despite-quorum-woes [Accessed: 5 May 2015].

b. Ensor, L., 2014. Withdrawal of Gender Equity Bill Welcomed, *Business Day Live* [online]. http://www.bdlive.co.za/business/2014/07/10/withdrawal-of-gender-equity-bill-welcomed [Accessed 5 May 2015].

Fallon, M.K., Swiss, L. & Viterna, J., 2012. Resolving the Democracy Paradox: Democratization and Women's Legislative Representation in Developing Nations, 1975 to 2009. *American Sociological Review*, 77(3), pp. 380-408.

Fein, H., 1999. Genocide and Gender: The Uses of Women and Group Destiny. *Journal of Genocide Research*, 1(1), pp. 43-63.

Fester, G., 2007. Rhetoric of Real Rights: Gender Equality in Africa, *Agenda: Empowering Women for Gender Equity*, 21(72), pp. 169-180.

Fraser, H., 2004. Doing Narrative Research: Analysing Personal Stories Line by Line. *Qualitative Social Work*, 3(2), 179-201.

Gaidzanwa, R.B.(2013). African Feminism. *Open Society Initiative for Souther Africa* [online]. Available at: http://www.osisa.org/sites/default/files/sup files/Africa%20Feminism%20-%20Rudo%20Gaidzanwa.pdf [Accessed 4 June 2015].

Geisler, G., 2000. "Parliament is Another Terrain of Struggle": Women, Men and Politics in South Africa. *The Journal of Modern African Studies*, 38(4), pp. 605–630.

Geisler, G., Mokgope, K. & Svanemyr, J., 2009. The National Gender Machinery, Gender Mainstreaming and the Fight Against Gender Based Violence. *African Development Bank & African Development Fund*.

Gender Links, 2012. The War @ Home: Findings of the Gender Based Violence Prevalence Study in Gauteng, Western Cape, KwaZulu Natal and Limpopo Provinces of South Africa. Available at: http://www.genderlinks.org.za/article/the-warhome-findings-of-the-gbv-prevalence-study-in-south-africa-2012-11-25 [Accessed: 5 May 2015].

Gender Links, 2014. South Africa Misses the Mark on Women in Politics. *Allafrica.com* [online]. Available at: http://allafrica.com/stories/201405271261.html [Accessed 19 February 2015].

Gerstel, N., 2000. The Third Shift: Gender and Care Work Outside the Home. *Qualitative Sociology*, 23(4), pp. 467–483.

Gallagher, E. & Delworth, U., 1993. The Third Shift. Juggling Employment, Family and the Farm. *Journal of Rural Community Psychology*, 12(2), pp. 21-36

Ginwala, F., Mackintosh, M. & Massey, D., 1990. Gender and Economic Policy in a Democratic South Africa. *Collected Seminar Papers. Institute of Commonwealth Studies*, 44, pp. 146-171.

Ginwala, F., 1990. Women and the African National Congress, 1912-1943. *Agenda: Empowering Women for Gender Equity*, 6(8), pp. 77-93.

Girls Education Movement, South Africa. Available at: http://library.unescoiicba.org/English/Girls%20Education/All%20Articles/General/Girls%20Education%20Movement%20South%20Africa%20Unicef.pdf [Accessed: 5 May 2015].

Gobodo-Madikizela, P., 2005. Women's Contributions to South Africa's Truth and Reconciliation Commission. *Women Waging Peace Policy Commission*.

Goetz, A.M. 1998. Women in Politics and Gender Equity in Policy: South Africa & Uganda, *Review of African Political Economy*, 25(76), pp. 241-262.

Goetz, A. M., 2003. Women's political effectiveness: A conceptual framework. In: Goetz, A.M. & Hassim, S. (eds.). *No Shortcuts to Power: African Women in Politics and Policy Making*, 1st ed. London: Zed Books

Goetz, A.M., Cueva-Beteta, H., Eddon, R., Sandler, J., Doraid, M., Bhandarkar, M., Anwar, S. & Dayal, A., 2009. Who Answers to Women? Gender & Accountability.

United Nations Development Fund for Women [online]. Available at: http://www.unifem.org/progress/2008 [Accessed 5 May 2015].

Goetz, A.M. & Hassim, S., 2003. Introduction: Women in Power in Uganda and South Africa, 1st ed. In: Goetz, A.M. & Hassim, S. (eds.). *No Shortcuts to Power: African Women in Politics and Policy Making*. London: Zed Books., pp. 1-28.

Goldblatt, B. & Meintjes, S., 1998. Dealing with the aftermath: sexual violence and the Truth and Reconciliation Commission. *Agenda: Empowering Women for Gender Equity*, 13(36), pp. 7–18.

Gouws, A., 1996. The Rise of the Femocrat? *Agenda: Empowering Women for Gender Equity*, 30, pp. 31-43.

Gouws, A., 2006. The State of the National Gender Machinery: Structural Probems and Personalised Politics. In: Buhlungu, S., Daniel, J., Southall, R. & Lutchman, J. (Ed.). (2006). *State of the Nation: South Africa, 2005-2006*. HSRC Press., pp. 143-168.

Gouws, A. & Kotzé, H., 2007. Women in Leadership Positions in South Africa: The Role of Values. *Politikon*, 34(2), pp. 165–185.

Graybill, L., 2001. The Contribution of The Truth and Reconciliation Commission Toward the Promotion of Women's Rights in South Africa. *Women's Studies International Forum*, 24(1), pp. 1–10.

Gertsel, N., 2000. The Third Shift: Gender and Care Work Outside the Home. *Qualitative Sociology*, 23(40), pp. 467-483.

Hassim, S., 1999. From Presence to Power: Women's Citizenship in a New Democracy. *Agenda: Empowering Women for Gender Equity*, 15(40), pp. 6-17.

Hassim, S., 2004. Nationalism, Feminism and Autonomy: The ANC in Exile and the Question of Women. *Journal of Southern African Studies*, 30(3), pp. 433–456.

Herndon, G. & Randell, S., 2013. Surviving Genocide, Thriving in Politics: Rwandan Women's Power. *Cosmopolitan Civil Societies Journal,* 5(1), pp. 69-96.

High-pippert, A. & Comer, J., 2008. Female Empowerment: The Influence of Women Representing Women. *Women & Politics*, 19(4), pp. 53-66.

Hinojosa, M., 2008. Mas Mujeres? Mexico's Mixed-Member Electoral System. In: Tremblay, M. (ed.). Women and Legislative Representation, 1st ed. Palgrave Macmillan, New York., pp. 177-190.

Hintjens, H.M., 1999. Explaining the 1994 genocide in Rwanda. *The Journal of Modern African Studies*, 37(2), pp. 241-286.

Hochschild, A., & Machung, A., 1990. The Second Shift: Working Families and the Revolution at Home. New York: Penguin.

Hochschild, A., 1997. The Time Bind, *WorkingUSA,* 1(2), pp. 21-29.

Hogg, C.L., 2010. Women's Political Representation in Post-Conflict Rwanda: A Politics of Inclusion or Exclusion? *Journal of International Women's Studies*, 11(3), pp. 34–55.

Hogg, N., 2010. Women's Participation in The Rwandan Genocide: Mothers or Monsters? *International Review of the Red Cross*, 92(877), pp. 69–102.

Hoogeveen, J.G. & Ozler, B., 2006. Not Separate, Not Equal: Poverty and Inequality in Post-Apartheid South Africa: 1995-2000. In: Bhorat, H. & Kanbur, R. (eds.) *Poverty and Policy in Post-Apartheid South Africa*, 1st ed. Cape Town: HSRC Press., pp. 59-94.

Inter-Parliamentary Union, 2015. Women in National Parliaments. Available at http://www.ipu.org/wmn-e/classif.htm [Accessed: 4 May 2015].

Jordan, B., 2014. 'Barbie', 'Nightgown' Jibes in Lindiwe Sisulu, Julius Malema Fashion War. *Times Live* [online]. Available at http://www.timeslive.co.za/politics/2014/07/21/barbie-nightgown-jibes-in-lindiwe-sisulu-julius-malema-fashion-war [Accessed: 4 May 2015].

Kantengwa, M.J., 2010. The Will to Political Power: Rwandan Women in Leadership. *IDS Bulletin*, 41(5), pp. 72–80.

Kayibanda, J.F., Bitera, R. & Alary, M., 2012. Violence Toward Women, Men's Sexual Risk Factors, and HIV Infection Among Women. *JAIDS Journal of Acquired Immune Deficiency Syndromes*, 59(3), pp. 300–307.

Kestelyn, I., 2010. *UNICEF's Work on Gender and Education in Rwanda*. UNICEF Rwanda, Commonwealth Education Partnerships.

Kramarae, C., 2000. *The Third Shift: Women Learning Online*. American Association of University Women Educational Foundation. Washington, D.C.

Krook, M.L., 2008. Quota Laws for Women in Politics: Implications for Feminist Practice. *Social Politics: International Studies in Gender, State & Society*, 15(3), pp. 345–368.

Kunovich, S.L., Paxton, P. & Hughes, M.M., 2007. Gender in Politics. *The Annual Review of Sociology*, 33, pp. 63–84.

Kwibuka, E., 2015. Full Pay for Maternity Leave Resumes in July. *The New Times* [online]. Available at: http://www.newtimes.co.rw/section/article/2015-03-24/187192/ [Accessed: 4 May 2015].

Lee, Y.G. & Hong, G.S., 2006. Third Shift Women in Business-Owning Families. *Journal of Family and Economic Issues*, 27(1), pp. 72–91.

Lodge, T., 1987. State of Exile: The African National Congress of South Africa. 1976-86. *Third World Quarterly*, 9(1), pp. 1–27.

Long, K., 2012. Rwanda's First Refugees: Tutsi Exile and International Response. *Journal of East African Studies, 6(2), pp.* 211-229.

Mabandla, B., 1994. Choices for South African Women. *Agenda: Empowering Women for Gender Equity*, 20, pp. 22-29.

Mack, N., Woodsong, C., MacQueen, K.M., Guest, G., Nancy, E., 2005. *Module 1: Qualitative Research Methods Overview*. Family Health International. Durham, United States.

Maier, D.J., 2013. Women Leaders in the Rwandan Genocide: When Women Choose To Kill. *Universitas,* 8, pp. 1-20.

Mail and Guardian, 2008. Zille Gives In and Admits to Botox. *Mail and Guardian* [online]. Available at: http://mg.co.za/article/2008-12-28-zille-gives-in-and-admits-to-botox [Accessed: 4 May 2015].

Martineau, R., 1997. Women and Education in South Africa: Factors Influencing Women's Educational Progress and their Entry into Traditionally Male-Dominated Fields. *Journal of Negro Education*, 66(4), pp. 383–395.

Mattina, G. La, 2014. Civil Conflict , Sex Ratio and Intimate Partner Violence in Rwanda. Allied Social Science Association Conference.

McLean Hilker, L., 2011. The Role of Education in Driving Conflict and Building Peace: The Case of Rwanda. *Prospects*, 41(2), pp. 267–282.

Van der Meeren, R., 1996. Three Decades in Exile: Rwandan Refugees 1960-1990. *Journal of Refugee Studies*, 9(3), pp. 252–267.

Meintjes, S., 2003. The politics of engagement: Women transforming the policy process– domestic violence legislation in South Africa, 1st ed. In: Goetz, A.M. & Hassim, S. (eds.). *No Shortcuts to Power: African Women in Politics and Policy Making*. London: Zed Books., pp. 140-159.

Molyneax, M., 1985. Mobilization without Emancipation? Women's Interests, the State, and Revolution in Nicaragua. *Feminist Studies*, 11(2), pp. 227-254.

Mtintso, T., 2003. Representivity: False Sisterhood or Universal WOmen's Interests? The South African Experience. *Feminist Studies*, 29(3), pp. 569-579.

Musoni, E., 2015. Behind Resignation of District Mayors. *The New Times* [online]. Available at: http://www.newtimes.co.rw/section/article/2015-01-05/184662/ [Accessed: 4 May 2015].

Newbury, B.D., 2001. Precolonial Burundi and Rwanda: Local Loyalties, Regional Royalties. *The International Journal of African Historical Studies*, 34(2), pp. 255–314.

Newbury, D., 2005. Returning Refugees: Four Historical Patterns of "Coming Home" to Rwanda. *Comparative Studies in Society and History*, 47(02), pp. 252–285.

News24.com, 2013. 'Angies' Panties' Heading for Court. Available at: http://www.news24.com/SouthAfrica/Politics/Angies-panties-heading-for-court-20130428 [Accessed: 4 May 2015].

News24.com, 2013. ANC Withdraws Mazibuko Weight Remark. Available at: http://www.news24.com/SouthAfrica/Politics/ANC-withdraws-Mazibuko-weight-remark-20130618 [Accessed: 4 May 2015].

News of Rwanda, 2015. Rwanda: Kagame Approves Bill Seeking 100 Percent Payment for Mothers on Maternity Leave. *AllAfrica.com*, [online]. Available at: http://allafrica.com/stories/201503240230.html [Accessed: 4 May 2015].

Ngendahimana, L., 2012. Imihigo: 6 Years of Transforming Rwanda. *The Independent*, [online]. Available at: http://www.independent.co.ug/supplement/117-supplement/6597-imihigo-six-years-of-transforming-rwanda [Accessed: 4 May 2015].

Paxton, P.M. & Kunovich, S., 2003. Women's Political Representation: The Importance of Ideology. *Social Forces*, 82(1), pp. 87–113.

Pitkin, H.F., 1967. *The Concept of Representation*. University of California Press.

Posel, D. & Rogan, M., 2012. Gendered trends in poverty in the post-apartheid period, 1997–2006. *Development Southern Africa*, 29(1), pp. 97–113.

Powley, E., 2004. *Strengthening Governance□: The Role of Women in Rwanda's Transition: A Summary*. United Nations. Office of the special adviser on gender issues and advancement of women (OSAGI).

Powley, E., 2006. *Rwanda: The impact of Women Legislators on Policy Outcomes*

Affecting Children and Families. United Nations Children's Fund.

Powley, E., 2005. Rwanda: Women hold up half the parliament. *Women in Parliament: Beyond Numbers*, pp. 154–163.

Reed, W.C., 1996. Exile, Reform, and the Rise of the Rwandan Patriotic Front. *The Journal of Modern African Studies*, 34(03), pp. 479-501.

Reyntjens, F., 2006. Post-1994 Politics in Rwanda: Problematising 'Liberation' and 'Democratisation'. *Third World Quarterly*, 27(6), pp. 1103-1117.

Reyntjens, F., 2010. Constructing the Truth, Dealing with Dissent, Domesticating the World: Governance in Post-Genocide Rwanda. *African Affairs*, pp. 1-34.

Rickets, E.A. 2013. Women's Access to Secondary Education in Colonial and Postcolonial Tanzania and Rwanda, Masters Dissertation. Loyola University Chicago.

Rwanda Governance Board (2014). Imihigo. Available at: http://www.independent.co.ug/supplement/117-supplement/6597-imihigo-six-years-of-transforming-rwanda [Accessed: 4 May 2015].

SabinetLaw, 2015. Women Empowerment and Gender Equality. Available at: http://www.sabinetlaw.co.za/social-affairs/legislation/women-empowerment-and-gender-equality [Accessed 4 May 2015].

Scharlach, L., 1999. Gender and Genocide in Rwanda: Women as Agents and Objects of Genocide. *Journal of Genocide Research*, 1(3), pp. 387-399.

Schindler, K., 2008. Time allocation, Gender and Norms: Evidence from Post-Genocide Rwanda. German Institute for Economic Research (DIW Berlin). Available at: http://www.socialpolitik.ovgu.de/sozialpolitik_media/paper_update/Schindler_Kati_ui d595_pid532-p-525.pdf [Accessed 5 May 2015].

Seager, J. (2006). The Penguin Atlas of Women in the World. 4th Edition. Penguin Books.

Seidman, G.W., 1999. Gendered Citizenship: South Africa's Democratic Transition and the Construction of a Gendered State. *Gender & Society*, 13(3), pp. 287–307.

South African History Online (2015). Congress of South African Students. Available at: http://www.sahistory.org.za/topic/congress-south-african-students-cosas [Accessed: 4 May 2015].

Stroh, A., 2010. Electoral Rules of The Authoritarian Game: Undemocratic Effects of Proportional Representation in Rwanda. *Journal of Eastern African Studies*, 4(1), pp. 1–19.

Suttner, R., 2003. Culture(s) of the African National Congress of South Africa: Imprint of Exile Experiences. *Journal of Contemporary African Studies*, 21(2), pp. 303–320.

The ACE Electoral Knowledge Network, 2015. Available at: http://aceproject.org/regions-en/countries-and-territories/RW [Accessed 10 June 2015].

The Citizen, 2014. Gender Bill 'Unrealistic' – Cape Chamber. Available at: http://citizen.co.za/119374/gender-bill-unrealistic-cape-chamber/ [Accessed: 5 May 2015].

The Constitution of the Republic of South Africa, 1996.

Thomas, D., 1996. Education Across Generations in South Africa. *The American Economic Review*, 86(2), pp. 330-334.

Tripp, A.M., No Date. *Why do Authoritarian Regimes Adopt Quotas: Lessons from*

African States. University of Wisconsin-Madison.

Tripp, A.M., 2003. The Changing Face of Africa's Legislatures: Women and Quotas, Paper presented at the International Institute for Democracy and Electoral Assistance, Electoral Institute of Southern Africa, Southern African Development Community Parliamentary Forum Conference.

Tripp, A.M. & Kang, A., 2008. The Global Impact of Quotas. On The Fast Track to Increased Female Legislative Representation. *Comparative Political Studies,* 41(3), pp. 338-361.

United Nations Rwanda, No Date. Country Assessment on Violence Against Women: Rwanda. Women Watch. Available at: http://www.un.org/womenwatch/ianwge/taskforces/vaw/VAW_COUNTRY_ASSESSME NT-Rwanda-1.pdf [Accessed: 5 May 2015].

Uwineza, P. & Pearson, E. 2009. Sustaining Women's Gains in Rwanda: The Influence of Indigenous Culture and Post-Genocide Politics. The Institute for Inclusive Security, Powley, E. (Ed.).

Waring, M., Greenwood, G. & Pintat, C., 2000. *Politics: Women's Insight.* Inter-Parliamentary Union.

Wolbrecht, C. and Campbell, D.E., 2013. Leading by Example□: Female Models of Parliament. *American Journal of Political Science,* 51(4), pp. 921–939.

Yoon, M.Y., 2001. Democratization and Women's Legislative Representation in Sub-Saharan Africa. *Democratization,* 8(2), pp. 169–190.

Yoon, M.Y., 2004. Explaining Women's Legislative Representation in Sub-Saharan Africa. *Legislative Studies Quarterly,* 29(3), pp. 447-468.

Zuckerman, E. & Greenberg, M., 2004. The Gender Dimensions of Post-Conflict Reconstruction: An Analytical Framework for Policymakers. *Gender & Development,* 12(3), pp. 70–82.

Index

30%

30%, 16, 18, 19, 22, 23, 25, 26, 44, 50, 67, 96, 111

A

Accountability, 51, 55, 58
African Development Bank, 40
African Development Fund, 40
African National Congress. *See* ANC
Agang, 23
ANC, 8, 9, 17, 18, 19, 20, 21, 22, 23, 24, 33, 37, 44, 53, 54, 59, 65, 66, 81, 82, 84, 87, 92, 104, 106, 122, 123, 132, 133, 140, 145
Angola, 122, 132
Anti-Apartheid, 8, 9, 105, 114, 121
Apartheid, 2
authoritarian regime, 12, 17, 50, 74, 79

B

Bantu Education, 98, 105
Beijing Declaration and Platform for Action, 15, *See* BPfA
Bill of Rights, 43, 54
Black Consciousness Movement, 107, 114
BPfA, 10, 38, 41

C

CEDAW, 10, 44
CGE, 39

childcare, 64, 125, 126, 128, 131, 132, 135, 137, 138, 140, 147, 150
civil society backgrounds, 117
class, 4, 8, 14, 27, 55, 71, 81, 82, 83, 86, 87, 92, 99, 103, 105, 108, 114, 117, 120, 131
Commercial Code, 46
Commission on Gender Equality. *See* CGE
Congo, 5, 68, 89, 99
Constitutional Commission, 43
constitutional quota, 17
Convention for a Democratic South Africa, 17
Convention on the Elimination of All Forms of Discrimination Against Women. *See* CEDAW
COSAS, 105, 114
critical actors, 62, 63
critical mass, 26, 31, 36, 50
culture, 5, 19, 47, 50, 52, 53, 56, 70, 128, 130, 131
Customary Marriages Act, 44

D

DA, 23, 45
Democratic Alliance, 23
Department of Education and Culture, 106
Department of Women, Children, and Persons with Disabilities, 39
Descriptive representation, 29

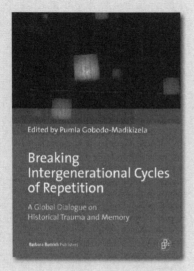

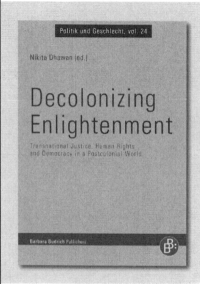